D1052736

Shakedown

SHAKEDOWN

The Continuing Conspiracy Against the American Taxpayer

Steven Malanga

Ivan R. Dee Chicago 2010

 For information, address: Ivan R. Dee, Publisher, 1332 North Halsted Street, Chicago 60642, a member of the Rowman & Littlefield Publishing Group. Manufactured in the United States of America and printed on acid-free paper.

www.ivanrdee.com

Most of the contents of this book appeared originally in *City Journal,* published by the Manhattan Institute.

Library of Congress Cataloging-in-Publication Data:
Malanga, Steven.
Shakedown : the continuing conspiracy against the American taxpayer / Steven Malanga.
p. cm.
Includes bibliographical references and index.
ISBN 978-1-56663-875-3 (cloth : alk. paper)
1. Government spending policy—United States. 2. Taxation—United States. 3. United States—Social policy—1993–
4. Government employee unions—United States. 5. Community activists—United States. I. Title.
HJ7537.M35 2010
336.73—dc22 2010010175

My thanks to Lawrence Mone, president of the Manhattan Institute, and the institute's staff and supporters, for allowing me to pursue the work that has resulted in this book. I'd also like to acknowledge the guidance and inspiration of Myron Magnet, former editor of City Journal, *and the current* City Journal *staff, especially Brian Anderson, for nurturing my work.*

Contents

Foreword

Steve Forbes

Here's a book that truly deserves those overused adjectives "timely" and "important." It enables us to grasp and analyze the root causes of the catastrophic financial collapse of so many state and local governments as well as the seemingly sudden explosion of federal spending and the unprecedented peace-time penetration of federal power into our now beleaguered free-enterprise economy. The economic crisis provided the pretext for Uncle Sam's neo-socialist power grab and laid bare the appalling weakness of much of our local government finance.

But these astonishing events have been a long time building. Steve Malanga incisively chronicles the rise of what he correctly labels the New New Left, starting with President Lyndon Johnson's War on Poverty in the 1960s. For the first time tax dollars were appropriated to ever more numerous and powerful pro-government pressure groups. What was—and still is—startlingly unique is that these organizations were not the traditional big-city political machines that did indeed use taxpayer money for corrupt purposes, that is, lining their pockets. Such old-time machines were ultimately accountable to voters—and to prosecutors. (The only meaningful survivor of these once-ubiquitous urban political powerhouses is Chicago's Daley machine, which, despite regular scandals, has prevented the Windy City from suffering the fate that blighted Detroit and other once mighty metropolises.)

But the New New Left doesn't have to face an electorate. Not until the Acorn scandals did it really feel the heat of the law for the all-too-often loose—nay, corrupt—way in which it handled its monies or fraudulently registered "new" voters or "got out the vote" for allegedly existing ones. Such pressure groups have also played a critical role in promoting public-sector unionization. And, in turn, the expanding unions have helped funnel more money to their Acorn-esque allies.

The New New Left has brilliantly exploited a vulnerability of democratic politics: Politicos respond to organized pressure groups that have the clout to either help or harm them. Steve Malanga tells the grim story of how such unions and their allies have financially undermined New Jersey, New York, and other political entities.

Fighting these tax-supported powers will be difficult. But the battle is essential if we are to save the very characteristics that have made this optimistic, opportunity-rich nation the inspiration to which Ronald Reagan so often and fondly referred when he called it that "shining city on the hill."

INTRODUCTION

The Conspiracy Against Taxpayers

IN VAULTING FROM Chicago precinct and ward politics into the presidency, Barack Obama represented the first appearance in the White House of a relatively new political type: the community organizer. Obama's ascendance was no anomaly, however. Although he boasted considerable political skills, his success in the 2008 presidential election was a testament to the rise of a powerful political coalition made up of those who benefit from expanding government: public-sector employees and their unions, activists at organizations that survive on government money, and recipients of government benefits. This self-interested coalition, which I dubbed the "New New Left" in my 2005 book of that name, has been amassing political power at taxpayer expense since the mid-1960s, when the War on Poverty fueled its rise. Obama's election was merely the clearest indicator of the extent to which the coalition has succeeded in changing politics in cities, states, and now in Washington.

The roots of community organizing go back to the 1930s and Chicago organizer Saul Alinsky, founder of the Industrial Areas Foundation and author of *Rules for Radicals*. But it wasn't until President Lyndon Johnson's ambitious plan to end poverty through massive federal spending that the Alinsky model—grassroots organizing, neighborhood by neighborhood—spread rapidly. Starting in the mid-sixties, as I outline in Chapter 5, the federal government directed billions of dollars to neighborhood groups, convinced that they knew better than Washington what their communities needed. The federal funds, eventually supplemented by state and local tax dollars, helped conjure into existence a universe of government-funded community groups that ran everything from job-training programs to voter-registration drives—far beyond anything Alinsky could have imagined. Some three thousand local social-services groups were soon receiving government funds in New York City alone. Many were new, but the money also helped transform traditional charities that had operated on private donations into government contractors.

Unsurprisingly, leaders of these social-services groups became advocates for government-funded solutions to social problems. To defend and expand their turf, organizers headed into the political arena, wielding the influence they had accumulated in neighborhoods to build bases of political support. In New York, operators of huge social-services groups like Pedro Espada in the Bronx and Albert Vann in Brooklyn won election to state and federal posts after heading up large, powerful nonprofits. By the late 1980s nearly 20 percent of New York City Council members were products of the government-funded nonprofit sector, and they proved strident advocates for higher taxes and ever more government spending. In cities from Chicago to Cleveland to Los Angeles, the road to electoral success increasingly ran through the government-funded social-services sector. Spending directed to these groups boomed through both Republican and Democratic administrations. "The non-profit service sector has never been richer, more powerful," former welfare recipient Theresa Funiciello wrote in her 1993 book *Tyranny of Kindness*. "Except to the poor, poverty is a mega-business."

Over time the advocates became expert at turning the machinery of government in their favor. In 1977, Congress passed the Community Reinvestment Act (CRA) at the urging of advocacy groups, who claimed that banks were "redlining"—that is, refusing to do business in many low-income neighborhoods. The legislation, described in Chapter 8, gave regulators the power to deny banks the right to expand if they didn't lend sufficiently in those neighborhoods, and eventually the government allowed community groups to protest bank applications to expand. To short-circuit these objections, banks shoveled money into programs administered by community activists. In 1993, for instance, fourteen major banks asked the controversial Association of Community Organizations for Reform Now (Acorn) to administer a $55 million, eleven-city lending program. In 2000 a U.S. Senate subcommittee estimated that CRA-related deals between banks and community groups pumped nearly $10 billion into the nonprofit sector.

Gradually the advocacy groups aligned with another rising player in the big-government coalition: public employees' unions, whose path to power began slowly in the late 1950s and early 1960s. For decades before that, government employees were protected by civil-service laws, but they had no collective bargaining rights. Often they could join organizations and professional groups that might testify and advocate on their behalf, but these groups couldn't call strikes or negotiate contracts for wages or benefits. That began to change in the mid-1950s, when the American Federation of State, County and Municipal Employees (AFSCME) persuaded New York City mayor Robert Wagner, who saw the Federation's members as potential political allies, to give municipal workers collective bargaining rights. Other states and cities quickly followed, as did the federal government in 1962.

These deals precipitated an era of turmoil. Government workers went on picket lines around the country in the 1960s; among the most visible examples were the dozens of teacher strikes that shut down big-city school systems. That prompted many states to rush out legislation forbidding public employees to strike. Blunted by the legislation and by rising anger at their growing militancy, public unions shifted tactics, concentrating their efforts in state capitols and municipal council chambers—and in local elections, where they ran grassroots efforts to select sympathetic political leaders. The unions were almost invariably advocates of bigger government and higher taxes, which swelled their ranks and increased their power, and soon they joined forces with the social-services groups—which, as we have seen, were seeking the same kind of expanding government.

This coalition successfully adopted the mantle of social justice to justify and promote its agenda, often with little opposition. The New New Left pushed living-wage laws, even when those laws were designed less to uplift low-wage workers than to increase union power by exempting from wage guidelines those firms that allowed workers to organize. The coalition decried efforts to eliminate spending programs like the federal Community Development Block Grants, claiming that such cuts would be attacks on the poor, even when there was little evidence that the patronage-riddled CDBGs did anything to alleviate poverty. The New New Left also belittled initiatives to restrain local property taxes as tantamount to attacks on schools and children, even where tax increases were spent on hefty wage and benefits gains for teachers, not on classrooms.

For a long time the power that these groups were gathering in cities and states was largely overlooked or dismissed as community politics. But by the dawn of the twenty-first century it became clear that the New New Left was more than just a local political movement. Politicians loyal to it had seized power in once-prosperous states like California and New Jersey, as I relate in Chapters 2 and 3, in the process transforming them into heavily taxed, heavily regulated, business-repellent environments where rich government salaries and pensions fueled continual budget crises. In 2004 this coalition also displayed its emerging national power, mustering enormous resources in an attempt to defeat George W. Bush's presidential reelection bid. Groups like AFSCME, the American Federation of Teachers, and the Service Employees International Union

(SEIU)—a former private-sector union that had transformed itself largely into a public-employee group—were among the largest contributors to a $65 million national advertising effort aimed at dethroning Bush. Although the president was reelected, the coalition had set the stage for an even bigger push four years later, when it helped one of their own win the Democratic presidential nomination and ultimately the 2008 general election.

Barack Obama began his organizing life in the mid-1980s in a community group whose progress mirrored that of the rest of the New New Left: the Developing Communities Project, formed on Chicago's South Side as a "faith-based grassroots organization organizing and advocating for social change." Although founded with resources from a coalition of churches, over time the DCP evolved, like many left-leaning religious organizations, into a government contractor essentially subsisting on tax money, with nearly 80 percent of its revenues derived from public contracts and grants.

As a young college graduate immersed in the world of tax-bankrolled activism, Obama reflected the big-government ethos that prevailed among neighborhood organizers who viewed attempts to reform poverty programs as attacks on the poor. "These are mean, cruel times, exemplified by a 'lock 'em up, take no prisoners' mentality that dominates the Republican-led Congress," Obama told an alternative weekly on the eve of his 1995 run for the Illinois state senate. He derided the "old individualistic bootstrap myth" of American achievement that conservatives were touting. Self-help strategies "have become thinly veiled excuses for cutting back on social programs, which are anathema to a conservative agenda," he wrote in a chapter he contributed to a 1990 book, *After Alinsky: Community Organizing in Illinois*. He also depicted leftist community organizing as a harder task than similar efforts by the Christian Right, telling a reporter in 1995: "It's always easier to organize around intolerance, narrow-mindedness and false nostalgia."

To maintain that society was fundamentally unjust, Obama had to deny the significance of the black advancement that surrounded him in Chicago. Looking out over the world of local politics in a city that until recently had been governed by a black mayor and had a number of prominent blacks in power, Obama saw only efforts to undermine African-American progress. In 1990 he did concede "black achievement in prominent city positions" but added that it had only "put us in the awkward position of administering underfunded systems neither equipped nor eager to address the needs of the urban poor." Still, Obama chose to head into politics himself, justifying the move as a third way between the limitations of local organizing and the narrow careerism that, he claimed, characterized local black pols. He, by contrast, would become the politician as community organizer.

Obama's legislative achievements as a state senator weren't extensive, but his supporters counted among his biggest victories his work to expand subsidized health care in Illinois, which he achieved in conjunction with social-justice groups like United Power for Action and Justice, an offshoot of Alinsky's Industrial Areas Foundation. Later, when he announced his run for president, Obama visited some of these groups and reminded them of their struggles together. Meeting with Acorn leaders, he declared: "I've been fighting alongside Acorn on issues you care about my entire career," including representing the group in a court case in Illinois. Acorn members apparently reciprocated by working hard to recruit voters for Obama's Illinois campaigns—according to a 2003 piece in the magazine *Social Policy* by a Chicago-area Acorn organizer—and then by endorsing him for the Democratic presidential nomination in 2008.

Obama's presidential campaign platform suggested that he continued to see the world through the eyes of a community organizer fighting the old War on Poverty, as I relate in Chapter 4. He touted programs to refuel the nonprofit sector, ranging from a commitment to boost money for federal relics (including that ineffective and wasteful Community Development Block Grant program) to a plan for "a full network of services, including early childhood education, youth violence prevention efforts and after-school activities . . . from birth to college" in a program he called "Promise Neighborhoods"—a sobriquet right out of the 1960s.

Once Obama became president, he quickly demonstrated how a member of the New New Left would govern. Early in his first term he funneled hundreds of billions of dollars of so-called stimulus money to states and cities to preserve government jobs. The money couldn't properly be justified as a stimulus under even the broadest definition of Keynesian economics, because funds spent on preserving government jobs produce virtually no additional multiplier effects elsewhere. Nonetheless the "stimulus" helped turn the national recession of 2008–2009 into a tale of two economies. During a tumultuous 2009 that saw the national unemployment rate rise to 10.6 percent, just 4.6 percent of government workers remained unemployed. Once, government workers had traded the higher wages and benefits they could earn in the private sector for job security in public service; nowadays, government employees get both job security *and* higher wages. As a 2005 study by the Employee Benefit Research Institute found, public-sector workers earned 46 percent more in salary and benefits than comparable private-sector workers. That gap has since grown larger: from the first quarter of 2007 through the last quarter of 2009, according to Josh Barro of the Manhattan Institute for Policy Research, the average value of hourly compensation (wages plus benefits) rose by 9.8 percent for employees of state and local governments, compared with 6.9 percent in the private sector.

The Obama administration went to extraordinary lengths to ensure that stimulus money was used to help its political allies. When California governor Arnold Schwarzenegger sensibly tried to lay off state workers during the state's 2009 budget crisis, Obama officials, at the behest of the SEIU, informed the state that it would forfeit hundreds of millions of stimulus dollars if it reduced its workforce. The Obama folks even—in a move that flabbergasted Schwarzenegger's staff—allowed SEIU reps to participate in the conference call in which California was read the riot act.

Another telling moment occurred early in Obama's first term when the White House crafted a deal to exempt unionized workers from a proposed tax on "Cadillac," or pricey, health-care plans. Portrayed as a victory for organized labor in general, the agreement was actually a gift to public-sector unions in particular, reflecting the rapidly changing nature of organized labor in America. The country had reached the point where more government workers than private workers were in unions, and these public employees typically held gold-plated health-benefits packages that were among the most expensive in America and far better than the modest benefits enjoyed by most private-sector union members. The unionized employees who would benefit disproportionately from the so-called Cadillac exemption would be public workers, not private ones.

The sharp public reaction against the cynical nature of the deal exemplifies the growing pains that the New New Left is experiencing as it goes national. But the coalition has adapted many times before, and it has tremendous resources at its disposal as well as a firm hold on the machinery of government at the state and local levels. That will make reform by taxpayers difficult and gradual at best. In *The New New Left* I showed how the big-government coalition had seized control of the politics of many cities and states and was trying to figure out how to go national. It succeeded more quickly than I could have imagined. Now it is taxpayers who are trying to figure out how to push back.

CHAPTER 1

The Bill Is Coming Due

FOR FIFTY YEARS, public unions, health-care lobbyists, and social-services advocacy groups have doggedly been amassing power in state capitols and city halls, using their influence to inflate pay and benefits for their workers and to boost government spending. The bill for that influence is now coming due, and it is overwhelming state and local budgets. For instance:

In New Jersey, legislators wooing union votes in 2001 voted a 9 percent hike in already rich pensions for the state's 500,000 public workers, even though a falling stock market was shrinking pension-fund assets. Those new perks have added billions of dollars to the state's deficit-ridden budgets since then.

In Washington State the powerful teachers' union led a successful 2000 effort to win legislation mandating smaller class sizes, promising that it would cost taxpayers nothing because surplus revenues could cover the program.

Instead the cash-strapped state passed $500 million in new taxes to finance the mandate.

In California, then-governor Gray Davis and a union-friendly state legislature passed a series of bills that swelled the number of state employees who could claim disability retirement benefits and also expanded the number of ailments automatically classed as job-related to include HIV, tuberculosis, and lower-back pain. The flood of new disability claims cost the state's retirement system some $465 million over five years, much of which came out of taxpayers' pockets.

Such extravagances help explain why state and local government spending reached an all-time high relative to the national GDP during the 2002 recession, producing a fiscal hangover that was only temporarily relieved by the financial bubble of 2006–2007 before revenues crashed again. These days, even in an expanding national economy, state and local budgets teeter in precarious balance, long-term deficits pile up, and politicians hike taxes to close spending gaps. The tidal wave of local government spending that produced these problems built up as tax revenues poured into state and municipal coffers during the 1990s boom. State tax collections rose by 86 percent, or about $250 billion, from 1990 through 2001, while local property-tax collections soared by $90 billion, or 60 percent, during a period when inflation increased by a mere 30 percent. Rather than give surpluses back to taxpayers, government went on a spree, lavishing opulent pensions on employees and expanding politically popular health and education programs.

All told, the swell of tax revenues produced about $93 billion in surpluses that state governments soaked up, according to Cato Institute estimates. State general-fund spending alone increased by 85 percent from 1990 to 2001, much faster than the combined rate of inflation and population growth. Absurdly, this spending tempo carried over into the economic slowdown that began in late 2001 and lingered into 2003, as budgets that appeared to be on autopilot grew rapidly, producing $85 billion in collective state budget deficits in fiscal 2003 alone. To close their budget gaps, state and local governments boosted taxes and fees on citizens and businesses already hurting from the economic downturn. Local property-tax bills, for instance, grew by about 6 percent a year from 2001 to 2004, even though the consumer price index increased by only 6.7 percent for the entire period.

The prime budget buster has been the wage and benefits packages of public employees. Contractually guaranteed, they are untouchable even during economic slowdowns. Public-employee unions have so successfully used their political muscle that where public-sector compensation once lagged the private sector, now the reverse is true. Astonishingly, the average state and local government employee now collects 46 percent more in total compensation (salary plus benefits) than the average private-sector employee, according to the nonpartisan Employee Benefit Research Institute.

Wages average a hefty 37 percent higher in the public sector, but the differences in benefits are even more dramatic. Local governments pay 128 percent more, on average, than private employers to finance workers' health-care benefits, and 162 percent more for retirement benefits. Although the private sector's heavier concentration of low-wage service employment accounts for some of the wage and benefit gap, public-sector employees do better these days even when you compare similar jobs. For example, total compensation among professional workers in the public sector is on average 11 percent higher than for similar jobs in the private sector.

Other comparisons of public- and private-sector pay illustrate the same gap. The Citizens Budget Commission, a New York City fiscal watchdog, found that the average public-sector worker in the metropolitan region received 15 percent more in pay (not including benefits) than the average private worker. The gap was greatest in service-sector jobs, like security guards, health-care workers, and building-maintenance workers, where government on average paid 94 percent more than private firms. A 2001 Rhode Island Public Expenditure Council comparison of private- and public-sector average wages across the nation found that the average public-sector wage was higher in thirty-five states.

The public unions were able to achieve this reversal only because government is a monopoly, exempt from marketplace discipline. Competition can punish private companies that give away the store to employees or that perform ineffectively, driving the most profligate or inefficient out of business. But government is perpetual regardless of how it performs, and public unions have succeeded over the years in layering new perks and benefits on top of previous collective-bargaining gains that rarely get rolled back, even in tough times. Awash in contributions from the unions and agencies whose pay they set, the gerrymandered state legislatures and one-party city halls that hand out such largesse are well insulated from voter retribution. Thus taxpayers wind up being nicked by a thousand small benefits piled upon one another year after year.

The buildup of two benefits in particular—pensions and health care—is now producing major budget disasters nationwide. State and local governments used tax surpluses and the 1990s stock-market rise to gold-plate pension programs, with disastrous effect once the stock boom ended. By 2003 state and local pension funds had accumulated more than $250 billion in unfunded liabilities, reports the National Association of State Retirement Administrators, leaving taxpayers on the hook. Pension costs in California's state budget skyrocketed fourteen-fold, from $160 million in 2000 to $2.6 billion in 2005, and are headed to $3.6 billion in 2010. New Jersey's pension costs are rising so quickly that without reform they will soon consume 20 percent of the state budget, up from 8 percent. Illinois' state budget pension obligations are on track to become a bigger part of the overall budget than local aid to education.

The pensions for which taxpayers must now foot the bill far outshine what many of those same taxpayers in the private sector receive. In New Jersey, for instance, a sixty-two-year-old state employee who retires after twenty-five years gets 50 percent more in yearly pension payments than an employee retiring with the same salary from the Camden, New Jersey, plant of Campbell Soup, a Fortune

500 company, according to the *Asbury Park Press*. In addition, the state employee receives free health insurance for life to supplement Medicare, while full health benefits for private-sector retirees are now rare. In California a public employee with thirty years of service can retire at fifty-five with 60 percent of his salary, and public-safety workers can get 90 percent of their salary at age fifty. By contrast with these rich payouts, the small (and shrinking) number of private firms that still provide "defined benefit" pension plans—instead of the now-common "defined contribution" plans that transfer all risk to the worker—pay on average 45 percent after thirty years of service.

Retired public employees in many states also get cost-of-living adjustments to their pensions, which those private-sector workers who still have defined benefit plans rarely enjoy. In Illinois, for instance, where pension payments increase by 3 percent each year—faster than the rate of inflation for most of the last decade—an employee who retired ten years ago with a monthly pension of $4,000 would now be collecting $5,400 a month.

Features unheard of in the private sector drive up government pension packages still further. In New York and Oregon, public employees who contribute their own money to retirement plans get a guaranteed rate of return that is often far beyond what the market provides, and taxpayers must make up the difference. In Oregon the return is 8 percent annually—about double what safe investments like treasury bonds provide today.

Rich health-care benefits have also added to a growing cost differential between the public and private sectors. The federal government's National Compensation Survey estimates that 60 percent of state and local employees have dental coverage, compared with 36 percent of private-sector workers, while 43 percent of local government workers have vision care included in their health plans, versus just 22 percent of private workers. More than 95 percent of state and local employees receive paid sick leave, but just 58 percent in the private sector do.

Yet even with states facing fiscal ruin, legislators continue to pour out new pension kickers and health benefits. In 2005 New Jersey lawmakers proposed eighty-six bills that would increase pension benefits, even though Acting Governor Richard Codey declared that "these entitlements are strangling the taxpayers of New Jersey." In Illinois, legislators trying to craft an early retirement plan several years ago to help meet the state's budget crisis so enriched the plan at the last minute that it cost about $200,000 per retiree instead of the projected $80,000.

Although union leaders defend these porcine compensation packages, claiming they help private workers by preventing a private-sector race to the bottom on wages and benefits, high public-sector pay is partly responsible for holding down private wages. Rhode Island is an especially telling example. The state ranks fourth in average pay in the public sector but only twenty-third in average private-sector wages, according to the Rhode Island Public Expenditure Council. To cover its high public-sector employee costs, Rhode Island has consistently raised taxes, giving it the sixth-highest total state and local tax burden in the country, including one of the highest corporate tax rates and sky-high property taxes. Those high taxes drain investment capital out of private-sector firms, making it harder for them to finance improvements that boost productivity, which is what in turn allows private-employee wages to rise. Rhode Island businesses have among the lowest rates of investment capital per employee in the country—30 percent below the national average. Thus the more the state enriches its public workers, the further its private workers—who pay public-sector salaries—fall behind. Rhode Island should serve as a cautionary tale for other states: it has one of the highest rates of unionization in the public sector—62 percent, compared with 37 percent nationally.

In this environment, public-sector retirees have become the haves and private retirees the new have-nots. When New Jersey's pension crisis hit, the state's newspapers began chronicling the flight of private-sector retirees to states where taxes are lower. Beset by its high public-sector costs, New Jersey has the highest combined state and local taxes in the country, and the fourth-highest level of migration of citizens to other states. One retiree from a manufacturing job told a local newspaper that he moved to Delaware so that he could reduce his property taxes from $3,300 a year in New Jersey to $615.

Yet public employees increasingly display a sense of entitlement about their rich benefits and pensions. Although the average public school teacher now retires at fifty-nine, and teachers work fewer months per year than private employees, attempts to raise teachers' retirement age to something closer to that of private-sector workers produce ominous warnings about shortages: "The idea of teaching until they are sixty-six makes many of our teachers wonder whether they want to be in this profession," a teachers' union lobbyist in Minnesota whined during a battle over pensions.

Thanks to union-friendly legislation that requires public school teachers to become members or pay dues even if they don't join, the size and wealth of teachers' unions have made them fiercely intimidating lobbying and electoral forces almost everywhere. In Pennsylvania a 1988 law requiring government employees to pay union fees helped double the size of the Pennsylvania State Education Association to 160,000 members, making it by far the most powerful lobbying force in the state, with 11 regional offices, 275 employees, and $66 million in annual dues. In California the state teachers' association collects a formidable $150 million a year in mandatory dues from 335,000 workers. The CTA can quickly raise additional funds in an emergency too, as when it hiked dues $60 a year to raise tens of millions more to fight Governor Schwarzenegger's special election.

Such resources have made teachers' unions among the biggest lobbyists and political givers at the state and local levels. The Wisconsin teachers' union plunked down a state-high $1.5 million for lobbying in Wisconsin's most recent legislative session, while Minnesota's union was number two in its state, spending nearly $1 million. Oregon's teachers' union, with $15 million in annual revenues, spent nearly $900,000 on political contributions in legislative races that helped Democrats gain control of the state's legislature and produced a union ex-president as the governor's education adviser. In New Jersey legislative elections, four-fifths of all incumbents received donations from the state's teachers' union.

In addition to higher wages and benefits, this megalobby increasingly has focused its might on schemes requiring big spending increases that will boost membership but are of dubious education value. A $2 million advertising campaign by California's teachers' union in the mid-1990s, for instance, won nearly $1 billion from the state government to cut class size, though considerable research shows that class-size reduction does little to improve student performance. The money set off a hiring frenzy that added thirty thousand teachers (and union members) in three years, but a Rand Corporation study found no significant change in test scores of students who wound up in smaller classes. The program's only tangible result is that those without full credentials jumped from 1.8 percent of all California teachers to 12.7 percent, as school districts snapped up warm bodies to obtain the extra state aid.

In Washington State too, the teachers' union pushed hard for class-size reduction as part of a package of bills that also mandated cost-of-living increases for teachers every year. When some legislators balked at the price tag, the union fired back with a $1.1 million ad campaign and a massive rally. The narrow election victory in 2004 of Governor Christine Gregoire, heavily supported by public unions, turned the tide in favor of the additional spending, prompting $500 million in state tax increases.

With no other group able to spend anywhere near so lavishly on education advocacy, voters now get most of their information from union lobbying and advertising. By relentlessly repeating the message that mean-spirited taxpayers shortchange America's kids, teachers' unions and education bureaucrats, with help from PTAs, have helped spread the myth that public schools are underfunded. An Educational Testing Services poll in 2004 found that nearly half of Americans think the schools spend on average just $5,000 per pupil a year—half the real amount.

Unions have also convinced Americans that teachers are underpaid, when they now take home considerably better pay packages on average than professional workers in the private sector. The federal government's national compensation survey estimates that local public school districts pay teachers an average of $47 per hour in total compensation, including $13 per hour in benefits—figures that far outstrip not only what private school teachers earn but also the average of what all professional workers earn in private business, a category that includes engineers, architects, computer scientists, lawyers, and journalists.

Teachers' unions use their power over state lawmakers to smother cost-saving reform ideas in their cradle. When school reformers sought support from Connecticut state legislators, they found teachers' union representatives camped outside the office of the legislature's education committee chair, keeping tabs on who met with him. When the Yankee Institute for Public Policy, a Hartford free-market think tank, held a media briefing on the state's budget, representatives of state-employee unions outnumbered the invited press. Institute board member George Schiele calls their pervasive presence in Hartford "Orwellian."

If state pols find teachers' unions so fearsome, little wonder that local school boards and municipal officials are no match for them at all. Lewis Andrews, a member of the

Redding, Connecticut, board of finance, had a glimpse of their raw power when he proposed an innovative alternative to the town's plans to expand its high school for a projected fifty-student enrollment increase. Supporters mailed a proposal to local residents, suggesting instead that the town pay to have fifty kids sent to private schools and save the millions on construction. The state's education lobby, which resists any program that smacks of privatization, went ballistic. "At eleven o'clock on the morning the proposal started arriving in the local mail, the president of the State Senate stormed into my office and started screaming at me about it," says Andrews. "I have no idea how they even found out about it so fast in the capitol." Needless to say, Redding expanded its high school.

Mario Mancieri, a Portsmouth, Rhode Island, school administrator for twenty-five years whose task it was to negotiate with the local teachers' union, made clear to the *Providence Journal* how outclassed local school boards and officials are when they go toe to toe with statewide teacher-bargaining units affiliated with a national organization. "As soon as one community picked up a benefit, it was only a matter of time before it would migrate to your community," he explained. At every contract discussion, the union made demands that extended a benefit in new and often unique ways. "In my community, sick days went from 12 to 15 to 20. . . . Then many teachers began complaining they didn't take their sick days. . . . So [they said,] 'I'd like to be paid for the days.' So we paid it out in dribs and drabs over the years." Resisting proved too costly. "We made every effort to hold the line," Mancieri recalled, "but strikes are devastating to the community, and we had three strikes." All this casts in a new light the No Child Left Behind Act's efforts to impose national accountability on an educational system whose management is local but whose employees are organized statewide and nationwide.

The education lobby's success most clearly shows up in the stunning growth of U.S. public education spending. In the last thirty years, per-pupil spending has nearly doubled, *after* accounting for inflation, to about $10,000 a year—far more than in most other industrialized countries, according to the Organisation for Economic Co-operation and Development, whose latest figures show that the United States outpaces Germany in per-pupil spending by 81 percent, France by 77 percent, and the United Kingdom by 20 percent. Even so, American students rank only in the middle of countries on student achievement tests, the OECD reports.

Municipalities have largely asked taxpayers to finance this spending through local property taxes. Since 1980, property-tax collections in the United States have increased more than fourfold, from $65 billion to about $275 billion—"only" a doubling after accounting for inflation. Collections have well outpaced the combination of population and inflation growth, according to the Tax Foundation, which found that from 1987 to 1997 per-capita local tax collections rose by more than 20 percent after inflation. The reason is clear: Pennsylvania's Commonwealth Foundation estimates that in the two decades before mandatory union dues, local property taxes in that state increased just 14 percent after inflation. But in the thirteen years after the 1988 legislation, property taxes went up 150 percent in real terms. Across the nation, much of that tax revenue has gone to finance new local education hires. In the 1990s local public education employment grew 24 percent, or by 1.4 million workers, in the United States.

But it's not just public employees like the teachers who have created a conspiracy against the taxpayers. Equally rapacious are the nominally private social-services and health-care providers who have found a way of diverting some of the torrent of government dollars to their own pockets. With so much money available from Medicaid, one of the original War on Poverty programs, health care has become an increasingly government-financed business and has been transformed unrecognizably in the process. Coalitions of hospital administrators, nursing-home operators, health-care unions, and advocacy groups—strange bedfellows indeed—have emerged as powerful state and local political players, using their muscle to extract ever higher Medicaid spending and more expansive coverage.

Since 2003 Medicaid has surpassed even education funding as the biggest state budget item. California spends nearly a third of its budget on subsidized health care, a 129 percent growth in the past decade. New York State's Medicaid budget not only constitutes 42 percent of state spending but also is now a larger budget item than education spending even for many of the state's county governments, which are forced to share Medicaid's costs (as is not the case in other states).

Health-care advocates insist that Medicaid spending is growing because of increasing need, but the numbers tell a different story. As tax revenues poured in during the 1990s, state politicians funneled the money into ever more generous programs. According to the Kaiser Family Foundation, two-thirds of Medicaid services that states now provide are optional under federal guidelines—from free ambulette rides to doctors' offices to dental and podiatry services. From 1994 to 2000, when U.S. poverty rates were plunging, spending on Medicaid, originally a program for the poor, grew by 30 percent after accounting for inflation, an American Enterprise Institute study shows. By contrast, Medicare spending, entirely controlled by the federal government, grew only half as fast, and total U.S. health-care spending increased by 18 percent after inflation.

While state officials now complain that they can no longer afford Medicaid programs they themselves have designed, they don't stop using them for political payoffs and patronage. An egregious case in point is home health care, originally a money-saving idea, transformed by political deals into a budget buster. States first expanded home care as a way of cutting nursing-home costs. Yet the strategy has backfired as unions, eyeing the proliferation of state-financed home-health-care workers, have organized them by the hundreds of thousands, pushing up their salaries and pensions while driving up union membership.

The Service Employees International Union's organizing of California's home-health-care workers in the 1980s is a textbook example. When the courts ruled that the workers were independent contractors who could not be organized, SEIU persuaded state legislators to pass a bill allowing counties to form authorities that could hire the workers as government employees, so that they could join the union. Then the union went to work in earnest to sign them up, including 74,000 in Los Angeles County alone—

the single largest successful union-organizing effort in the United States since the United Auto Workers organized General Motors in 1937.

To help finance higher pay for these workers, the union then turned back to Sacramento, persuading legislators to vote millions in aid to the counties. Although in 1998 Governor Pete Wilson vetoed the legislation as too expensive, the next year new governor Gray Davis—who had received $600,000 in campaign contributions from SEIU, his biggest supporter—signed the law. Since then the state's home-health-care spending has increased at nearly triple the rate of caseloads, costing taxpayers an additional three-quarters of a billion dollars. Local budgets are also straining under the pressure. Home-health-care-worker costs rose above $300 million a year and became the fastest-growing part of Los Angeles County's budget.

SEIU has managed to exploit other well-intentioned Medicaid programs for its own purposes. Washington State, for example, hoping to encourage family members to care for sick relatives at home, decided to allow Medicaid to pay family members or friends of recipients a nominal, state-subsidized fee to care for them, and such caregivers now account for about two-thirds of the state's subsidized home-health-care workers. But SEIU, sensing opportunity, campaigned for the right to organize these caregivers, eventually spending $1 million on a ballot initiative that had little formal opposition because few understood its implications and because no other special interest would lose from the legislation—just the taxpayer. When SEIU then successfully signed up the program's 26,000 workers, doubling the union's state membership, it demanded big increases in salaries as well as health and pension benefits. One local newspaper even quoted a newly organized mother whom the state was now paying to care for her retarded son as saying, without irony, "We need a decent wage."

With so much power and money at stake, health care is witnessing the transformation of former professional organizations into militant unions, as happened earlier to the National Education Association. The bellicose California Nurses Association, for instance, used its vocal opposition to Governor Schwarzenegger as a springboard to national organizing. The union won a political prize in 1999 when Governor Davis and the Democratic-controlled legislature mandated that hospitals have a five-to-one ratio of nurses to patients, despite warnings from hospitals that the law would cost the state's health-care system $1 billion annually and be virtually impossible to implement because of a nursing shortage. Governor Schwarzenegger, responding to reports that hospitals were closing down emergency rooms and wards because they couldn't meet the staffing demands, delayed implementation of the ratios for three years, igniting a firestorm. The union followed him on dozens of out-of-state visits to picket his appearances, hired a blimp to fly over a Super Bowl party at his private residence, and spent $100,000 on ads attacking his decision.

Hardly a collection of Florence Nightingales, the union hired a former Teamsters organizer as its chief in 1993, and she began a long process of making it over, ending its affiliation with the American Nurses Association and allying it instead with the Teamsters. Since then the organization has developed dreams of replacing the ANA around the country, using its victory on the California nurse-ratio issue as a recruiting tool in places like Hawaii, Michigan, Georgia, Arizona, and Illinois. Its rough-and-tumble tactics stand in stark contrast to those of professional nursing groups. The National Labor Relations Board overturned one of the union's organizing campaigns because members menaced anti-union nurses, showing up at the home of one opponent and telling him that his "little kittens would look good in a frying pan."

Such tactics are especially unsettling in health care. Even worse, when a Connecticut local affiliated with SEIU went on strike against nursing homes, workers engaged in vandalism and sabotage aimed at patients, according to an investigation by the state's attorney, including removing identification bracelets from Alzheimer's patients, feeding chocolate to diabetics, and loosening bolts on lifts used to support patients.

Government spending has bred strange alliances as unions and managements put aside their differences to lobby for more public money. In Illinois, Maryland, and Ohio, for example, the nation's largest operator of private nursing homes, Trans Healthcare, Inc., struck an agreement with SEIU locals not to oppose organizing efforts at its facilities if the union would help it lobby for higher Medicaid reimbursements. Together the two groups created a separate lobbying arm, financed with a $100,000 union contribution and a company pledge to match that amount.

In New York an alliance of Local 1199/SEIU and the Greater New York Hospital Association has used its hefty financial resources and political clout to propel the state's Medicaid budget, already the nation's biggest, to stratospheric heights. In 1999 a joint union-hospital group spent $13 million—the largest sum ever for a state lobbying campaign—on a successful effort not only to derail Governor Pataki's Medicaid reform efforts but also to press the state to pour billions from its share of the federal tobacco settlement into expanding the program. The coalition's attack ads, warning of hospital closings and other dire consequences, were so outrageous that even other hospital organizations complained about them. But no group in the state (besides taxpayers) had enough of an interest in stopping the alliance's campaign, so the ads went largely unchallenged.

Unsurprisingly, the unions and nonprofit hospitals that have flourished in the shower of government money don't want any private-sector competition. In Rhode Island, for instance, unions joined with doctors and local hospitals to oppose the entry of for-profit hospitals into the state, arguing that nonprofits are more altruistic and more faithful to their mission than profit-making hospitals. This contention ignores the fact that nonprofit hospital executives often pocket huge salaries and that subsidized nonprofits without bottom-line motivation often become inefficient and offer overly costly care. Nonetheless the coalition managed to push through one of the country's strictest hospital takeover laws, barring for-profits from entering Rhode Island on the grounds that they funnel money out of health care to investors. Now Rhode Island is paying the price for its unwise policy. Far from siphoning money out of health care, for-profit hospitals can use their ability to raise money in the capital markets to invest in new technologies and facilities, exactly what Rhode Island needs, since it is beset by "an aging hospital infrastructure that requires significant investment," according to a state health-care group.

Faced by the alliance between publicly funded employees and state legislators who have gerrymandered their districts to protect themselves from the wrath of voters, reformers are at a disadvantage. In Washington State, when voters rejected a ballot initiative to raise the state's sales tax to pay for smaller class sizes in 2004, the legislature went ahead and paid for the expense anyway, by using fiscal gimmicks to ram the state's annual spending right through the limit set by the voters more than a decade earlier.

Even so, the growing cost of state and local government has helped spark the stirrings of what could be the next great taxpayer revolt. Ballot initiatives seeking to cap local government growth or restrain public union powers proliferate, and reform candidates like New Jersey Republican Chris Christie run on a platform of smaller government. The stirrings of change are also evident in the so-called Tea Party anti-tax movement which, though focused on national politics, constitutes a series of local organizations slowly turning their attention to state and local issues.

But public-sector forces have spent the last fifty years gathering power and organizing effectively, and reform will not come easily.

CHAPTER 2

California's Road to Serfdom

THE CAMERA FOCUSES on an official of the Service Employees International Union (SEIU), California's largest public employees' union, sitting in a legislative chamber and speaking into a microphone. "We helped to get you into office, and we got a good memory," she says matter-of-factly to the elected officials outside the shot. "Come November, if you don't back our program, we'll get you out of office."

The video has become a sensation among California taxpayer groups for its vivid depiction of the audacious power that public-sector unions wield in their state. The unions' political triumphs have molded a California in which government workers thrive at the expense of a struggling private sector. The state's public school teachers are the highest-paid in the nation. Its prison guards can easily earn six-figure salaries. State workers routinely retire at fifty-five with pensions higher than their base pay for most of their working life. Meanwhile, what was once the most prosperous state now suffers from an unemployment rate far steeper than the nation's and from a flood of firms and jobs fleeing high taxes and stifling regulations. This toxic combination—high public-sector employee costs and sagging economic fortunes—has produced recurring budget crises in Sacramento and in virtually every municipality in the state.

How public employees became members of the elite class in a declining California offers a cautionary tale to the rest of the country. The story starts half a century ago, when California public workers won bargaining rights and quickly learned how to elect their own bosses—that is, sympathetic politicians who would grant them outsize pay and benefits in exchange for their support. Over time the unions have turned the state's politics completely in their favor. The result: unaffordable benefits for civil servants; fiscal chaos in Sacramento and in cities and towns across the state; and angry taxpayers finally confronting the unionized masters of California's unsustainable government.

California's government workers took longer than many of their counterparts to win the right to bargain collectively. New York City mayor Robert Wagner started a national movement back in the late 1950s when he granted negotiating rights to government unions, hoping to enlist them as allies against the city's Tammany Hall machine. The movement intensified in the early sixties after President John F. Kennedy conferred the right to bargain collectively on federal workers. In California, a more politically conservative environment at the time, public employees remained without negotiating power through most of the sixties, though they could join labor associations. In 1968, however, the state legislature passed the Meyers-Milias-Brown Act, extending bargaining rights to local government workers. Teachers and other state employees won the same rights in the seventies.

These legislative victories happened at a time of surging prosperity. California's aerospace industry, fueled by the cold war, was booming; investments in water supply and infrastructure nourished the state's agribusiness; cheaper air travel and a famously temperate climate burnished tourism. The twin lures of an expanding job market and rising incomes pushed the state's population higher, from about 16 million in 1960 to 23 million in 1980 and nearly 30 million by 1990. This expanding population in turn led to rapid growth in government jobs—from a mere 874,000 in 1960 to 1.76 million by 1980 and nearly 2.1 million in 1990—and to exploding public-union membership. In the late 1970s the California teachers' union boasted about 170,000 members; that number jumped to about 225,000 in the early 1990s and stands at 340,000 today.

The swelling government payroll made many California taxpayers uneasy, eventually encouraging the 1978 passage of Proposition 13, the famous initiative that capped property-tax hikes and sought to slow the growth of local governments, which feed on property taxes. Government workers rightly saw Prop 13 as a threat. "We're not going to just lie back and take it," a California labor leader told the *Washington Post* after the vote, adding that Prop 13 had made the union "more militant." The next several years proved him right. In 1980 alone, unionized employees of California local governments went on strike forty times, even though doing so was illegal. And once the Supreme Court of California sanctioned state and local workers' right to strike in 1985—something their counterparts in most other states still lack—the unions quickly mastered confrontational techniques like the "rolling strike," in which groups of workers walk off jobs at unannounced times, and the "blue flu," in which public-safety workers call in sick en masse.

At the same time, aware that Proposition 13 had shifted political action to the state capitol, three major blocs—teachers' unions, public safety unions, and the Service Employees International Union, which now represents 350,000 assorted government workers—began amassing colossal power in Sacramento. Over the last thirty years they have become elite political givers and the state's most powerful lobbying factions, replacing traditional interest groups and changing the balance of power. Today they vie for the title of most powerful political force in California.

Consider the California Teachers Association. Much of the CTA's clout derives from the fact that, like all government unions, it can help elect the very politicians who negotiate and approve its members' salaries and benefits. Soon after Prop 13 became law, the union launched a coordinated statewide effort to support friendly candidates in school-board races, in which turnout is frequently low and special interests can enjoy a disproportionate influence. In often bitter campaigns, union-backed candidates began sweeping out independent board members. By 1987 even conservative-leaning Orange County saw 83 percent of open board seats going to union-backed candidates. The resulting change in school-board composition made the boards close allies of the CTA.

But with union dues somewhere north of $1,000 per member and 340,000 members, the CTA can afford to be a player not just in local elections but in Sacramento too (and in Washington, for that matter, where it's the National Education Association's most powerful affiliate). The CTA entered the big time in 1988 when it almost singlehandedly led a statewide push to pass Proposition 98, an initiative—opposed by taxpayer groups and Governor George Deukmejian—that required 40 percent of the state's budget to fund local education. To drum up sympathy, the CTA ran controversial ads featuring students; in one, a first grader stares somberly into the camera and says, "Pay attention—today's lesson is about the school funding initiative." Victory brought local schools some $450 million a year in new funding, much of it discretionary. Unsurprisingly, the union-backed school boards often used the extra cash to fatten teachers' salaries—one reason why California's teachers are the country's highest paid, even though the state's total spending per student is only slightly higher than the national average. "The problem is that there is no organized constituency for parents and students in California," says Lanny Ebenstein, a former member of the Santa Barbara Board of Education and an economics professor at the University of California at Santa Barbara. "No one says to a board of education, 'We want more of that money to go for classrooms, for equipment.'"

With its growing financial strength, the CTA gained the ability to shape public opinion. In 1996, for instance, the union—casting covetous eyes on surplus tax revenues from the state's economic boom—spent $1 million on an ad campaign advocating smaller classes. Californians began seeing the state's classrooms as overcrowded, according to polls. So Governor Pete Wilson earmarked some three-quarters of a billion dollars annually to cut class sizes in kindergarten through third grade. The move produced no discernible improvements in student performance, but it did require a hiring spree that inflated CTA rolls and produced a teacher shortage. (The union drew the line, however, when it faced the threat of increased accountability. Two years later when Wilson offered funds to reduce class sizes even further but attached the money to new oversight mechanisms, the CTA spent $6 million to defeat the measure, living up to Wilson's assessment of it as a "relentless political machine.")

During this contentious period the CTA and its local affiliates learned to play hardball, frequently shutting down classes with strikes. The state estimated that in 1989 alone these strikes cost California students collectively some 7.2 million classroom days. Los Angeles teachers provoked outrage that year by reportedly urging their students to support the strikes by skipping school. After journalist Debra Saunders noted in the *Los Angeles Daily News* that the teachers were already well paid, the union published her home phone number in its newsletter and urged members to call her. The union was enraged that Saunders had pointed out to readers that the Los Angeles Board of Education was devoting virtually all the state education aid it received from the California lottery to teacher salaries.

Four years later the CTA reached new heights of thuggishness after a business-backed group began a petition to place a school-choice initiative on the state ballot.

Prompted by the union, teachers shadowed signature gatherers in shopping malls and aggressively dissuaded people from signing up. The tactic led to more than forty confrontations and protests of harassment by signature gatherers. "They get in between the signer and the petition," the head of the initiative said. "They scream at people. They threaten people." CTA's top official later justified the bullying: some ideas, he said, "are so evil that they should never even be presented to the voters."

The rise of the white-collar CTA provides a good example of a fundamental political shift that took place everywhere in the labor movement. In the aftermath of World War II, at the height of its influence, organized labor was dominated by private workers; as a result, union members were often culturally conservative and economically pro-growth. But as government workers have come to dominate the movement, it has moved left. By the mid-nineties the CTA was supporting causes well beyond its purview as a collective bargaining agent for teachers. In 1994, for instance, it opposed an initiative that prohibited illegal immigrants from using state government programs and another that banned the state from recognizing gay marriages performed elsewhere. Some union members began to complain that their dues were helping advance a political agenda that they disagreed with. "They take our money and spend it as they see fit," says Larry Sand, the founder of the California Teachers Empowerment Network, an organization of teachers and former teachers opposed to the CTA's noneducational politicking.

Public-safety workers—from cops and sheriffs to prison guards and highway-patrol officers—are the second part of the public-union triumvirate ruling California. In a state that has embraced some of the toughest criminal laws in the country, police and prison guards' unions own a precious currency: their political endorsements, which are highly sought after by candidates wanting to look tough on crime. But the qualification that the unions usually seek in candidates isn't, in fact, toughness on crime; it's a willingness to back better pay and benefits for public-safety workers.

The pattern was set in 1972 when State Assemblyman E. Richard Barnes—an archconservative former navy chaplain who had fought pension and fringe-benefit enhancements sought by government workers, including police officers and firefighters—ran for reelection. Barnes had one of the toughest records on crime of any state legislator. Yet cops and firefighters walked his district telling voters that he was soft on criminals. He narrowly lost. As the *Orange County Register* observed years later, the election sent a message to all legislators that resonates even today: "Your career is at risk if you dare fiddle with police and fire" pay and benefits.

The state's prison guards' union has exploited a similar message. Back in 1980 when the California Correctional Peace Officers Association (CCPOA) won the right to represent prison guards in contract negotiations, it was a small fraternal organization of some 1,600 members. But as California's inmate population surged and the state went on a prison-building spree—constructing 22 new institutions over 25 years—union membership expanded to 17,000 in 1988, 25,000 by 1997, and 31,000 today. Union resources rose correspondingly, with a budget soaring to

$25 million or so, supporting a staff 70 deep, including 20 lawyers.

Deploying these resources, the union began to go after politicians who didn't support higher salaries and benefits for its members and an ever-expanding prison system. In 2004, for example, the CCPOA spent $200,000—a whopping amount for a state assembly race—to unseat Republican Phil Wyman of Tehachapi. His sin: advocating the privatization of some state prisons in order to save money. "The amount of money that unions are pouring into local races is staggering," says Joe Armendariz, executive director of the Santa Barbara County Taxpayers Association. A recent mayoral and city council election in Santa Barbara, with a population of just ninety thousand, cost more than $1 million, he observes.

The symbiotic relationship between the CCPOA and former governor Gray Davis provides a remarkable example of the union's power. In 1998 when Davis first ran for governor, the union threw him its endorsement. Along with those much-needed law-and-order credentials, it also gave Davis $1.5 million in campaign contributions and another $1 million in independent ads supporting him. Four years later, as Davis geared up for reelection, he awarded the CCPOA a stunning 34 percent pay hike over five years, increasing the average base salary of a California prison guard from about $50,000 a year to $65,000—and this at a time when the unemployment rate in the state had been rising for nearly a year and a half and government revenues had been falling. The deal cost the state budget an additional $2 billion over the life of the contract. A union official described it admiringly as "the best labor contract in the history of California." Eight weeks after the offer, the union donated $1 million to Davis's reelection campaign.

Even cops who run for office have felt the wrath of public-safety unions. Allan Mansoor served sixteen years as a deputy sheriff in Orange County but angered police unions by publicly backing an initiative that would have required them to gain their members' permission to spend dues on political activities. When the conservative Mansoor ran for the Costa Mesa city council, local cops and firefighters had poured resources into helping his more liberal opponents. "I didn't like seeing my dues go to candidates like Davis, so I supported efforts to curb that," Mansoor says. "Union leaders didn't like it, so they endorsed my opponents by claiming they were tougher on crime than I was."

Even more troubling are the activities of the California Organization of Police and Sheriffs (COPS), a lobbying and advocacy group that has raised tens of millions of dollars from controversial soliciting campaigns. In one, COPS fund-raisers reportedly threatened to cut off residents' 911 services unless they donated. In another a COPS fund-raiser reportedly offered to shave points off Californians' driving records in exchange for donations. The group has dunned politicians too. In 1998 it began publishing a voter guide in which candidates paid to be included. Pols considered the money well spent because of the importance of a COPS endorsement—or at least the appearance of one. "We all use them [COPS] for cover, especially in years when law enforcement is a big issue in elections," one state senator, Santa Clara's John Vasconcellos, admitted to the

Orange County Register. "It stopped the right wing from calling me soft on crime."

The results of union pressure are clear. In most states, cops and other safety officers can typically retire at fifty with a pension of about half their final working salary; in California they often receive 90 percent of their pay if they retire at the same age. The state's munificent disability system lets public-safety workers retire with rich pay for a range of ailments that have nothing to do with their jobs, costing taxpayers hundreds of millions of dollars. California's prison guards are the nation's highest paid, a big reason that spending on the state's prison system has blasted from less than 4.3 percent of the budget in 1986 to more than 11 percent today.

California's third big public-union player is the state wing of the SEIU, the nation's fastest-growing union, whose chief, Andy Stern, earned notoriety by visiting the White House twenty-two times during the first six months of the Obama administration. Founded in 1921 as a janitors' union, the SEIU slowly transformed itself into a labor group representing government and health-care workers—especially health-care workers paid by government medical programs like Medicaid. In 1984 the California State Employees Association, which represented many state workers, decided to affiliate with the SEIU. Today the SEIU represents 700,000 California workers—more than a third of its nationwide membership. Of those, 350,000 are government employees: noninstructional workers in schools across the state; all nonpublic safety workers in California's burgeoning prisons; 2,000 doctors, mostly residents and interns, at state-run hospitals; and many others at the local, county, and state levels.

The SEIU's rise in California illustrates again how modern labor's biggest victories take place in back rooms, not on picket lines. In the late 1980s the SEIU began eyeing a huge jackpot: tens of thousands of home-health-care workers being paid by California's county-run Medicaid programs. The SEIU initiated a long legal effort to have those workers, who were independent contractors, declared government employees. When the courts finally agreed, the union went about organizing them—an easy task because governments rarely contest organizing campaigns, not wanting to seem anti-worker. The SEIU's greatest victory was winning representation for 74,000 home-health-care workers in Los Angeles County, the largest single organizing drive since the United Auto Workers unionized General Motors in 1937. Taxpayers paid a steep price: home-health-care costs became the fastest-growing part of the Los Angeles County budget after the SEIU bargained for higher wages and benefits for these new recruits. The SEIU also organized home-care workers in several other counties, reaching a whopping statewide total of 130,000 new members.

The SEIU's California numbers have given it extraordinary resources to pour into political campaigns. The union's major locals contributed $20 million in 2005 to defeat a series of initiatives to cap government growth and rein in union power. The SEIU has also spent millions over the years on initiatives to increase taxes, sometimes failing but on other occasions succeeding, as with a 2004 measure to impose a millionaires' tax to finance more mental-health spending. With an overflowing war chest and hundreds of thousands of foot soldiers, the SEIU has been instrumental in persuading local governments to pass living-wage laws in several California cities, including Los Angeles and San Francisco. And the union has also wielded its muscle in campaigns largely out of the public eye, as in 2003, when it pressured the board of CALPERS, the giant California public-employee pension fund, to stop investing in companies that outsourced government jobs to private contractors.

ARMED WITH KNOWLEDGE about California's three public-union heavyweights, one can begin to understand how the state found itself in its nightmarish fiscal situation. The beginning of the end was the 1998 gubernatorial election, in which the unions bet their future—and millions of dollars in members' dues—on Gray Davis. The candidate traveled to the SEIU's headquarters to remind it of his support during earlier battles against GOP governors ("Nobody in this race has done anywhere near as much as I have for SEIU"); the union responded by pumping $600,000 into his campaign. Declaring himself the "education candidate" who would expand funding of public education, Davis received $1.2 million from the CTA. Added to this was Davis's success in winning away from Republicans key public-safety endorsements—and millions in contributions—from the likes of the CCPOA.

Davis's subsequent victory over Republican Dan Lungren afforded public-worker unions a unique opportunity to cash in the IOUs they had accumulated, because Davis's Democratic party also controlled the state legislature.

What followed was a series of breathtaking deals that left California state and municipal governments careening from one budget crisis to another for the next decade.

Perhaps the most costly was far-reaching 1999 legislation that wildly increased pension benefits for state employees. It included an unprecedented retroactive cost-of-living adjustment for the already retired and the phaseout of a cheaper pension plan that Governor Wilson had instituted in 1991. The deal also granted public-safety workers the right to retire at fifty with 90 percent of their salary. To justify the incredible enhancements, Davis and the legislature turned to CALPERS, whose board was stocked with members either aligned with unions or appointed by state officials who themselves were elected with union help. The CALPERS board, which had lobbied for the pension bill, issued a preposterous opinion that the state could provide the new benefits mostly out of the pension systems' existing surplus and future stock-market gains. Most California municipalities soon followed the state enhancements for their own pension deals.

When the stock market slid in 2000, state and local governments were slammed with enormous bills for pension benefits. The state's annual share, estimated by CALPERS back in 1999 to be only a few hundred million dollars, reached $3 billion by 2010. Counties and municipalities were no better off. Orange County's retirement system saw its payouts to retirees jump to $410 million a year by 2009, from $140 million a decade ago. Many legislators who had voted for the pension legislation (including all but seven Republicans) later claimed that they'd had no idea its fiscal impact would be so devastating. They had swallowed the rosy CALPERS projections even though they knew very well that the board was, as one county budget chief put it, "the fox in the henhouse."

The second budget-busting deal of the Davis era was the work of the teachers' union. In 2000 the CTA began lobbying to have a chunk of the state's budget surplus devoted to education. In a massive rally in Sacramento, thousands of teachers gathered on the steps of the capitol, some chanting for TV cameras, "We want money! We want money!" Behind the scenes, Davis kept up running negotiations with the union over just how big the pot should be. "While you were on your way to Sacramento, I was driving there the evening of May 7, and the governor and I talked three times on my cell phone," CTA president Wayne Johnson later boasted to members. "The first call was just general conversation. The second call, he had an offer of $1.2 billion. . . . On the third call, he upped the ante to $1.5 billion." Finally, in meetings, both sides agreed on $1.84 billion. As *Sacramento Bee* columnist Dan Walters later observed, that deal didn't merely help blow the state's surplus; it also locked in higher baseline spending for education. The result: "When revenues returned to normal, the state faced a deficit that eventually not only cost Davis his governorship in 2003 but has plagued his successor, Arnold Schwarzenegger."

Having wielded so much power effortlessly, the unions miscalculated the anti-tax, anti-Davis sentiment that erupted when, shortly after his fall 2002 reelection, Davis announced that the state faced a massive deficit. The budget surprise spurred an enormous effort to recall Davis, which the unions worked to defeat, with the SEIU alone spending $2 million. At the same time union leaders used their muscle in the Democratic party to try to save Davis, telling other Democrats that they would receive no union support if they abandoned the governor. "If you betray us, we won't forget it," the head of the 800,000-member Los Angeles County Federation of Labor proclaimed to Democrats. Only when it became apparent from polls that the recall would succeed did the unions shift their support to Lieutenant Governor Cruz Bustamante, who finished a distant second to Schwarzenegger. Taxpayer groups were euphoric.

But as they and Schwarzenegger soon discovered, most of California's government machinery remained union controlled—especially the Democratic state legislature, which blocked long-term reform. Frustrated, Schwarzenegger backed a series of 2005 initiatives sponsored by taxpayer groups to curb the unions and restrain government growth, including one proposal that made it harder for public-employee unions to use members' dues for political purposes. The controversial proposals sparked the most expensive statewide election in American history. Advocacy groups and businesses spent a staggering $300 million (some of it, however, coming from drug companies trying to head off an unrelated initiative). The spending spree included $57 million from the CTA, which mortgaged its Sacramento headquarters for the cause. All the initiatives went down to defeat.

California taxpayers nevertheless received a brief respite, thanks to the mid-decade housing boom that drove the economy and tax collections higher and momentarily eased the state's budget crunch. Predictably, state politicians forgot California's Davis-era deficit woes and gobbled up the surpluses, increasing spending by 32 percent, or $34 billion, in four years. Then the housing market crashed in 2007, prompting a cascade of budget crises in Sacramento and around the state. Only too late have Californians recognized the true magnitude of their fiscal problems, including a $21 billion deficit by mid-2009 that forced the state to issue IOUs when it temporarily ran out of cash. In the municipal bond market, fears are rising that the Golden State might default on its debt.

Public unions and their defenders have tried to blame their continuing fiscal mess on Proposition 13, the 1978 law limiting property tax hikes, but a thorough look at taxes in California belies that explanation. As Claremont McKenna College economist William Voegeli has pointed out in *City Journal*, California state and local governments have instituted many other taxes and fees as sources of revenues since 1978, so that according to the 2007 census report on governmental expenditures, the state ranks fifth in the nation in government income per capita, and fourth in state and local spending per capita. That hardly represents a state starved for revenues by Proposition 13, as unions and politicians like former governor Davis suggest.

Municipalities around the state are also buckling under massive labor costs. One city, Vallejo, has already filed for bankruptcy to get out from under onerous employee salaries and pension obligations. (To stop other cities from going this route, unions are promoting a new law to make it harder for municipalities to declare bankruptcy.) Other local California governments, big and small, are nearing disaster. The city of Orange, with a budget of just $88 million in 2009, spent $13 million of it on pensions and expects that figure to rise to $23 million in just three years. Contra Costa's pension costs rose from $70 million in 2000 to $200 million by the end of the decade, producing a budget crisis. Los Angeles, where payroll constitutes nearly half the city's $7 billion budget, faces budget shortfalls of hundreds of millions of dollars next year, projected to grow to $1 billion annually in several years. (In October 2007, even as it was clear that the area's housing economy was crashing, city officials had handed out 23 percent raises to workers over a five-year period.)

"When you have a system where unions can contribute heavily to elect the people who pay them, corruption is inevitable," says Mark Bucher, founder of the Education Alliance, a group that tries to help elect candidates who are independent of unions.

In the past, California could always rely on a rebounding economy to save it from its budgetary excesses. But these days few view the state as the land of opportunity. Throughout the national recession that began in December 2008 and carried through 2009, California's unemployment rate consistently ran several points higher than the national rate. Major California companies like Google and Intel have chosen to expand elsewhere, not in their home state. Put off by the high taxes and cumbersome regulatory regime that the public-sector cartel has led the way in foisting on the state, executives now view California as a noxious business environment. In a 2008 survey by a consulting group, Development Counsellors International, business executives rated California the state where they were least likely to locate new operations.

More and more California taxpayers are realizing how the system is stacked against them. They are also coming to understand that reform will come slowly, if it comes at all.

CHAPTER 3

The Mob That Whacked Jersey

WHEN CY THANNIKARY left India to come work at the United Nations in Manhattan, he settled in Flushing, Queens, and loved the excitement of living in the city. After starting a family, though, he traded New York's hubbub for Freehold, New Jersey, a quiet suburb with lower taxes and affordable housing. That was twenty-five years ago. These days Thannikary sometimes feels like he's back in Gotham as he watches his taxes soar and hears neighbors grumble. He has started a new taxpayer group to fight the special interests that have turned both state and local government into profligate spenders. "Politicians in New Jersey have treated their citizens as ATMs," he complains. "They have no idea how to restrain spending, and more and more people are saying they can't afford to live here anymore."

For more than a century and a half, New Jersey, nestled between New York City and Philadelphia, offered commuters like Thannikary affordable living in pleasant communities. Wall Street tycoons, middle managers fleeing high-priced Gotham once they'd married and had kids, and immigrants who settled first in New York but quickly discovered that they could pursue the American dream more easily across the Hudson—all flocked into the Garden State. Eventually New Jersey's congenial living attracted even corporations escaping New York's rising crime and taxes. The state flourished.

But today Jersey is a cautionary example of how to cripple a thriving state. Increasingly muscular public-sector unions have won billions in outlandish benefits and wages from compliant officeholders. A powerful public education cartel has driven school spending skyward, making Jersey among the nation's biggest education spenders, even as student achievement lags. Inept, often corrupt, politicians have squandered yet more billions wrung from suburban taxpayers, supposedly to uplift the poor in the state's troubled cities, which have nevertheless continued to crumble despite the record spending. To fund this extravagance, the state has relentlessly raised taxes on both residents and businesses while localities have jacked up property taxes furiously. Jersey's cost advantage over its free-spending neighbors has vanished: it is now among the nation's most heavily taxed places. And despite the extra levies, the state has faced perpetual budget crises, even during the best of times.

Unless Garden State leaders can stand up to entrenched interests, the state may find itself permanently relegated to second-class economic status. New Jersey "could become the next California, with budget problems too big to solve without a lot of pain," warns former Jersey City mayor

Bret Schundler. "The old way of raising taxes to solve budget problems has been tried, and it's done nothing but make things worse."

Once a farming corridor connecting New York and Philadelphia, the state that Benjamin Franklin called "a keg tapped at both ends" began its rapid evolution in the nineteenth century, spurred by the growth of the railroads. Enterprising New Yorkers like the merchant Matthias Ogden Halsted led the way. In 1837 he repossessed a one-hundred-acre farm in Orange, New Jersey—about twelve miles west of Manhattan—and built a magnificent mansion, featuring Corinthian columns that one historian celebrated as "unlike anything the area had ever seen." He subdivided the rest of the farm to provide homes for city friends. These new suburban commuters even chipped in to help build a railway station on the nearby Lackawanna train line, a stop that still serves commuters today.

In 1853, following Halsted's example, Manhattan drug wholesaler Llewellyn Solomon Haskell bought land along a ridge of the Orange Mountains, laid down roads, and built grand homes. Thus was born Llewellyn Park, America's first gated community. Described by the *New York Times* in 1865 as "a rough, shaggy mountain site, now transformed into an enchanted ground," Llewellyn Park soon attracted such eminent residents as Thomas Edison, and it boasted magnificent houses designed by noted architects, including Stanford White, Charles McKim, and Calvert Vaux. Soon the entire area around the Oranges blossomed, with stylish homes on broad boulevards. Fashionable New York stores like B. Altman and Best &

Co. turned the area's dazzling main shopping strip into the rightly nicknamed "Fifth Avenue of the suburbs."

Jersey's development accelerated during the second half of the nineteenth and the early twentieth centuries as more and more workers opted for suburban comfort. A new railroad line here, a bridge or road there, would unlock a whole new swath of the state to commuters, igniting countless mini-real-estate booms.

Two rail lines transformed Montclair in the mid-nineteenth century from a sleepy trading post into a bustling New York commuter town, filled with spacious Tudor- and Queen Anne–style homes. Montclair's biggest houses, on a ridge at the foot of the Watchung Mountains facing New York, would one day house many of Gotham's financial elite, including, during the late 1980s, the chief executives of three of Manhattan's biggest banks. In the same fashion a causeway over the Shrewsbury River in 1870, linking farmland communities like Fair Haven and Rumson to ferries on the Atlantic, prompted a number of New York financiers, including Jacob Schiff, to build estates in the area and begin commuting across New York harbor to work.

Some sixty miles north of Rumson and fifty years later, construction of the George Washington Bridge, connecting upper Manhattan and the Bronx to northern New Jersey, led to a different kind of housing boom in places like Teaneck, a middle-class town where developers erected English Tudors, Dutch Colonials, and smaller houses of stucco and brick. In the decade leading up to the bridge's opening, Teaneck's population grew fourfold, part of a population upsurge that remade northern Jersey.

As inexpensive mass transportation expanded, New Jersey sprouted a dense network of middle-class suburbs, home to many Manhattan middle managers—the traders, back-office managers, and salesmen who serve as corporate New York's foot soldiers. In the 1960s the Levitt family, famous for converting Long Island farmland into the middle-class suburb of Levittown after World War II, replicated the project on a more modest scale in Somerset, New Jersey, building nearly 1,000 houses in William Levitt's classic Cape Cod design. Middle-income New Yorkers came in droves. Farther north, in Hillsdale, where the Hackensack & New York Railroad once had a terminus, hundreds of modest two- and three-bedroom prewar colonial houses, originally built for railroad workers, formed the core of a housing market dominated by Manhattan commuters. Eisenhower-era ranch houses in Middleton, Morristown townhouse developments, condos on former industrial land in Jersey City and Secaucus—all attracted commuters, so that now more than 300,000 Gotham workers call New Jersey home.

New Jersey would even cultivate its own patrician dynasties of Gothamites. Shortly before launching the New York–based financial magazine bearing his name in 1917, B. C. Forbes moved his family from Bay Ridge, Brooklyn, to Englewood, New Jersey, on the western slope of the Palisades. After his magazine took off and Forbes became prominent within Englewood—by then home to many of Manhattan's financial elite—his son Malcolm married one of the town's finest, Roberta Laidlaw, whose family owned the New York investment firm Laidlaw & Co. The pair moved into a baronial estate in the rolling hills of

Somerset County, deep in the Jersey heartland. Among their neighbors: Aristotle and Jacqueline Kennedy Onassis, former secretary of state Cyrus Vance, and longtime Dillon Read chairman and ex–treasury secretary Douglas Dillon.

The commuters have helped give New Jersey the highest average family income in the country. In one five-year period during the mid-1990s, the state had a net gain of $2.8 billion in family income from New York, thanks to between-state migration, the Empire State Foundation found.

The ex–New Yorkers who formed the New Jersey towns favored small government and low taxes, which came to define the state's politics. As early as 1840 the mayor of Jersey City—then a settlement of just over three thousand—boasted of his town's "small amount of taxes levied to support state, county, and city government compared to New York and Brooklyn" (an independent municipality at the time). Jerseyans could be downright ornery about taxation. During the depression the state's Republican governor, Harold Hoffman, enacted a sales tax; so great was the backlash that the legislature quickly rescinded the levy. By the early 1960s New Jersey was one of only two states without a sales or an income tax; New York had both. New Jersey ranked fortieth among states in total tax burden, 13 percent below the national average.

The presence of a white-collar commuting workforce—and the low-tax economic climate it helped create—would help New Jersey lure firms fleeing New York. By 1910 more than half the state's urban and suburban residents worked in office jobs, as clerks, typists, managers, and executives.

When Gotham's corporations, at first seeking space and then, beginning in the sixties, pushed by high taxes and escalating crime, began to abandon the city, New Jersey was an attractive option. AT&T, Chubb Insurance, American Standard, Bristol-Myers Squibb, and others began flocking to where many of their employees already lived. Technological advances also helped New Jersey draw the back-office operations of major finance players like Merrill Lynch, which kept its Manhattan headquarters but now employed thousands of support workers in cheaper Garden State digs, connected by phone and computer.

The New York corporate exiles nourished New Jersey's economy, just as the commuters did. Starting in the 1950s, New Jersey's economy began growing at twice the pace of New York State's and easily outperformed it for most of the rest of the century. Even in finance, New York City's economic engine, New Jersey has almost matched Gotham's growth in recent decades. Between 1970 and 2000 it added 143,000 financial-sector jobs, compared with 154,000 new jobs in New York City over the same period, as financial wizards no longer chose only to live in the Garden State but also to work there. Even soon-to-be New York mayor Michael Bloomberg got in on the action. From a small Princeton office in the late 1980s, the mayor's company, Bloomberg LP, grew to employ 1,500 in New Jersey by the early twenty-first century.

The features that lured commuters and firms to the Garden State began slowly to erode in the late 1960s, as an expanding state government started shoveling massive amounts of taxpayer money into urban anti-poverty programs and education, usually with little result. Two interlocking forces drove the spending: first, the rise of powerful public-sector unions that pushed effectively for higher pay and benefits, bloating municipal and school budgets and blocking needed reforms not just in cities but across the state; second, the growth in New Jersey cities of a new kind of political machine that diverted federal and state urban aid into political favors and patronage, wasting billions on useless and often crooked programs, and turning the cities into expensive wards of the state.

Until the 1960s New Jersey's cities, though small, had been self-sustaining and relatively successful, playing a minor role in the larger regional economy governed by New York. Newark, for instance, became a port town, with a small manufacturing hub that, at its peak in 1930, employed some 66,000 workers of the city's 450,000 inhabitants. But when race riots and unrest broke out in Newark, Camden, and other New Jersey cities during the late 1960s, many residents and businesses fled to the same suburbs that New Yorkers had been flooding into for decades. Cities like Newark ended up with little economic life and mostly indigent populations.

Further encouraging the exodus was a widespread awareness that the cities had fallen into the grip of corrupt, rapacious political machines. After Newark's riots, federal prosecutors bore down on then-mayor Hugh Addonizio, who had given control of much of the city to Mafia bosses Ruggiero "Richie the Boot" Boiardo (whose crime family inspired *The Sopranos*) and Ray DeCarlo. After the feds convicted Addonizio and several subordinates for corruption, the "reformers" who took over were anything but. New mayor Kenneth Gibson, pledging to end the sleaze and revive Newark, faced ceaseless investigations into his administration, resulting in a string of indictments—including his own on charges of providing a no-show job. Although never convicted, Gibson left office a failure.

Corruption probes into the administration of the next mayor, Sharpe James, over nearly twenty years brought down city councilmen, the mayor's own chief of staff, and the police commissioner, who pled guilty in 1996 to pillaging a fund that financed undercover narcotics investigations. Nor was Camden any less shady: since 1981 three of its mayors have been convicted of corruption and deposed.

The persistent corruption, vaporizing billions of taxpayer dollars, gave public-sector unions the leverage to wrest control of the state's urban agenda for their own benefit, leading to even greater waste. Newark's teachers' union, for example, used Gibson's legal woes to seize control of the schools from the mayor and deliver it to a school board—which the union, with more than four thousand voting members, could easily elect. The result: a long period of school-system mismanagement and fraud, documented in a damning 1994 state investigation, which culminated in state takeover of the system the next year. In his book *Black Mayors and School Politics*, political scientist Wilbur Rich blames the school failure on "the public education cartel" and says that claims by teachers and board members that poverty caused the system to fail "is an insult to the Newark community."

New Jersey's cities have never recovered. Newark now has only 280,000 residents, down from 450,000 in happier times. State taxpayers pay about three-quarters of a billion dollars annually to prop up the city's schools and its municipal government. Crime is rampant, jobs scarce. Newark's problems have radiated to neighboring towns too, blighting once-healthy communities. Irvington, which Philip Roth in *Portnoy's Complaint* depicted as filled with alluring *shiksas* living in Norman Rockwellesque tranquillity, is today one of New Jersey's poorest communities, wracked by double-digit unemployment and a crime rate as bad as Newark's.

In Camden, the nation's murder capital, the state had to take over the failed school system and the city's out-of-control finances. Trenton, Paterson, and other New Jersey cities are similarly dysfunctional.

The latest installment of this ruinously expensive mess is a court-ordered state effort to rebuild dysfunctional urban school systems. In a series of decisions beginning in the 1990s, the New Jersey Supreme Court has forced the state to boost spending dramatically in city schools. Going beyond fiscal equity cases in other states, which demand that prosperous suburban residents contribute more to poor urban school systems, the New Jersey supremes mandated that each district be able to spend as much as the state's richest jurisdictions—up to $25,000 per pupil. The court also required the state to establish universal preschool and to embark on a $2 billion school building program.

Once the courts decreed this modern-day exercise in taxation without representation, union-backed pols piled on. In 2001 the state legislature inflated the school construction program to a budget-busting $8.6 billion—a gift not only to the education lobby but also to the construction unions. To evade voter approval (which the state constitution requires) for the lavish spending, the legislature created a largely unaccountable bond-issuing authority, a constitutional dodge that Jersey's courts blessed. The patronage-ridden authority proved so corrupt that it quickly spent all its borrowed money while completing only half its building projects, leaving taxpayers under court order to pour in yet more funds.

By the 2003–2004 school year, state taxpayers, in a colossal income transfer, were handing over a jaw-dropping $4 billion annually to support education spending in Jersey cities. Taxpayers from elsewhere in the state footed fully 90 percent of Camden's education bill while the city itself contributed a mere 2 percent, says the school reform group EducateNJ. In Trenton, state taxpayers paid 82 percent of the education bill; local sources ponied up just 8 percent.

Yet even as Garden State taxpayers have showered nearly $30 billion on city schools, neither the courts nor the officials overseeing the urban school districts have demanded fundamental reform of the school bureaucracies, let alone innovative solutions like vouchers. The money thus has made little difference. True, state tests show a recent uptick in fourth-grade reading and math proficiency (though little gain for eighth graders and high school students). But the improvements, such as they are, result at least partially from the state dumbing down its tests over the last few years. Soberingly, on national tests, New Jersey students show insignificant gains for all grade levels since 1992 and considerably lower levels of math and reading proficiency than the state tests claim.

In state legislative testimony, the vice president of Newark's Public School Advisory Board starkly framed the lack of progress. "There has been little, if any, real success that the minority and low-income children of my city can claim," she said, thanks to the "abysmal failure of our system." In Camden and Newark that system spends nearly $1 billion in state funds annually—to produce a scant two thousand high school grads a year.

It's hard to overstate the might that public-sector unions—the teachers' union, above all—now wield in New Jersey. With 62 percent of its state and local workers organized, New Jersey has the second-highest level of public-sector unionization in the country, behind only New York, according to unionstats.com.

The unions have wielded their clout to win among the richest benefits and highest pay of government workers anywhere. Teachers earn an average of $60,000 a year, with some of the highest salaries going to teachers in the state-financed urban districts. Not only are health and pension benefits for state workers—including the possibility of retiring at fifty-five with cost-of-living pension adjustments for life—plusher than the private-sector norm; on average, they're 10 to 15 percent above what other state governments grant workers. By 2008 the tab grew to nearly $5 billion, and by 2010, $6.7 billion—21 percent of the projected state budget.

The unions ferociously protect their spoils. The New Jersey Education Association was the prime mover of a $300,000 ad campaign opposing a thus-far-unsuccessful effort by taxpayer groups to call a constitutional convention to fix Jersey's tax woes. Facing taxpayer pressure, the state legislature took up a bill to limit annual school spending hikes to 2.5 percent, or the rate of inflation, whichever was less. The teachers' union leaned on legislators and got the word "less" changed to "greater," inverting the bill's intent. The Communications Workers of America, representing government employees, strongly backed a recent $1 billion increase in taxes on Jersey businesses, running radio ads demanding that firms pay their "fair share."

All the union- and court-driven spending and misspending has burdened New Jersey citizens and firms with heavy taxes and led to a multi-billion-dollar redistribution of income from suburban counties to the state's urban core—and from private to public employees. New Jersey's wealth belt—six adjacent counties in the state's center (Hunterdon, Mercer, Middlesex, Monmouth, Morris, and Somerset)—handed over $4.2 billion in sales and income taxes in 2003 but got just $2.2 billion back from the state in spending, a Rutgers University study found. By contrast, New Jersey's most urban counties—Camden, Essex, Hudson, Passaic—paid $1.6 billion in taxes in 2003 but enjoyed $3.6 billion in aid.

New Jersey's progressive income tax accounts for much of this skewed distribution. Statewide, families making $150,000 a year or more are just 9 percent of tax filers but pay 55 percent of income taxes—a percentage likely to rise after the levying of a so-called millionaires' tax that hiked rates for residents making $500,000 or more, giving them a top rate of nearly 9 percent. (Neighboring Pennsylvania has a flat 3.07 percent rate for all taxpayers.)

Since their residents get precious little in return for their state taxes, most of Jersey's suburban governments must finance their operations through property taxes—one reason those taxes are the nation's highest, according to the Tax Foundation. Today New Jersey suburbanites find themselves paying for *two* sets of local governments and *two* school systems: their own (through property taxes) and those of cities like Camden and Newark (through income and sales taxes).

Many ordinary, hardworking New Jersey residents feel like the taxman won't rest until he's pushed them out of the state. Citizens for Property Tax Reform member Jo-Anne David lives in a small duplex on a three-thousand-foot lot in rural Jamesburg but pays some $5,000 a year in property taxes. She bluntly sums up her situation: "I can't wait to retire and get out of this state. I can't afford to live here, and it's a shame." Leaving New Jersey has become the sensible option for middle-class retirees, says Lou Albright of suburban Gloucester Township. "I have lived and worked in New Jersey all my life and now in retirement can no longer afford to live here," he observes. "In so many ways the state tells you when you have completed your working life: We don't want you—move on to Delaware or some other tax-friendly state."

Hefty tax hikes are also leading many New York workers to reconsider their choice to live in Jersey. When Jerry Cantrell moved to Randolph, New Jersey, from a Pennsylvania suburb so that his wife could take a New York corporate job, he knew that his property taxes would go up—from $1,800 in Pennsylvania to $5,000 in Jersey. But he didn't expect them to keep rising—nearly 50 percent in just ten years, so that he now shells out nearly $7,500 a year. "Somehow you don't believe they can keep going up so much," complains Cantrell, who leads the Silver Brigade, another taxpayer rights group. Cantrell has gotten more than he bargained for in Jersey in other ways. After leading a campaign to defeat a $45 million school building plan that the local education establishment supported, he had his house pelted with eggs and found threatening notes stuffed in his mailbox.

New Jersey's taxes have arced upward for forty years, interrupted only briefly by then-governor Christine Todd Whitman's mid-1990s income tax cuts. Despite her helpful tax cuts, Whitman contributed to the state's long-term problems when she used fiscal gimmicks to pay for rising state pensions that masked the true cost of the benefits to taxpayers, just as her Republican predecessor in the 1980s, Governor Tom Kean, had allowed state spending to rise robustly during the era's prosperity. To continue funding this expansive government once the economy slowed starting in 2002, the new Democratic governor, James McGreevey, boosted state taxes strongly after his party seized control of the legislature. McGreevey jacked up taxes and fees thirty-three times—totaling a whopping $3.6 billion—during his short tenure, which ended in less than three years after the public learned that he had given a state job to his purported homosexual lover. Although his new "millionaires' tax" got most of the attention, the middle class has taken a hard hit. McGreevey hugely hiked the tax on home sales, for instance, affecting some 140,000 families yearly, most of them middle class. A New Jerseyan who sells his $450,000 home must now pay a whopping $3,695 tax, an 80 percent increase; selling a modest $300,000 house would require shelling out $2,200, a 72 percent hike.

Under McGreevey, New Jersey also instituted its own estate tax, kicking in at $675,000 in assets, well below the starting point for the federal death tax. Perhaps to protect its residents from dying with too much wealth, the state also raised taxes on retirees with $100,000 or more in annual income, charging them extra to help pay public-sector retirees.

Spending as wildly as he taxed, McGreevey borrowed nearly $2 billion to finance a colossal 17 percent increase in his last budget. Although the state supreme court judged that move unconstitutional, it let the action stand because the money had already been appropriated.

Such reckless taxing and spending intensified the flight out of the Garden State, which has one of the highest levels of out-migration among the states. In 2004 alone, New Jersey netted a loss of more than $1 billion in personal income from out-migration, according to Internal Revenue Service data. "Jersey has blown a golden opportunity," says former Republican presidential candidate Steve Forbes, a resident of Far Hills, New Jersey. "It could have been like Hong Kong, a haven for wealth and industry among high-tax neighbors like New York. Instead, Jersey's now losing its own residents to places like North Carolina."

McGreevey also chilled the state's already inhospitable business climate. He boosted corporate taxes and ended the ability of struggling companies to deduct losses from their tax bills—one of the most ruinous corporate tax schemes in the nation. When the head of Cincinnati-based Federated Department Stores, one of New Jersey's biggest employers, noted that its state tax bill would more than double (to $10 million) and that it would reconsider any further expansion in the state, McGreevey attacked the company, challenging it to slash executive pay. His tax regime "drastically alters New Jersey's corporate tax landscape, making it inhospitable to large corporations," observed Glenn Newman, former deputy commissioner in New York City's Department of Finance.

Meanwhile Democratic legislative leaders installed as heads of the assembly and senate labor committees two lawmakers who also are union officials—thereby putting labor legislation into the hands of union bosses. Since then the legislature has passed draconian new laws that require companies on public projects to pay union wages and that subject violators to *criminal* charges, not just civil fines. New Jersey solons have also passed an "instant unionization" bill that lets union locals organize workplaces simply by getting a majority of workers to sign cards—no need for a secret ballot anymore. "It seems Trenton looks for ways to discourage firms from moving here or expanding here," corporate CEO Fred Barré told a gathering of the state's manufacturers.

Not surprisingly, a place that big employers once viewed as a safe haven now ranks low on the list of places to do business. The Beacon Hill Institute, an economic research group, ranked New Jersey as the seventh-worst state in the country for business—and noted that it had fallen more than any state since its previous survey a couple of years earlier. The Tax Foundation finds the state's business-tax burden the country's second-worst. Economy.com calculates the cost of doing business there the third-highest in the United States.

The higher taxes and a tangle of new regulations have nearly halted what was once a regional jobs locomotive. Although the state's economy easily outperformed the rest of its region for the past fifty years (and occasionally even outpaced the nation), it grew at only half its 1990s rate, and only one-third the rate of its 1980s boom, during the robust national expansion of the early twenty-first century. In a 2004 report, Rutgers economists James Hughes and Joseph Seneca identified as a chief culprit in New Jersey's economic decline the state's "recent intense focus on income redistribution."

Faced with these burdens, New Jersey voters nonetheless turned to U.S. Senator Jon Corzine, who, heavily backed by public-sector interests, won the state's 2005 gubernatorial election. During his five years as U.S. senator from New Jersey, the former Wall Street executive was consistently one of the Senate's most liberal members, with a long record of favoring higher taxes and greater spending. He won the 2005 Jersey gubernatorial election on a platform that promised more than $1 billion in tax relief to property owners, but he identified no significant cuts in state spending to free up that revenue. The money would come from revenue growth, he claimed—an unrealistic goal in a state with a struggling economy and a colossal deficit. Faced with the reality of governing, Corzine acknowledged that the state's fiscal condition was worse than he thought, and his advisers began floating tax increases as a solution. He raised the state's sales tax by $1 billion, promising the money would go to property tax relief, but when the national recession hit Corzine eventually suspended property tax rebates for most residents, leaving them with his big tax increase but little tax relief.

At that point even New Jersey voters grew frustrated. Despite an enormous effort to reelect Corzine, heavily supported by the powerful New Jersey Education Association, Republican Chris Christie defeated Corzine on a platform to cut taxes and spending and especially to reform overly generous public-employee pensions.

But he is sure to face a challenge from the state's muscular public unions, which fought fiercely against his candidacy and which still have enormous influence in the Democratic-controlled legislature. As Christie and the state's taxpayers have discovered since the last big taxpayer revolt of the early 1990s, their opponents, especially the public-sector unions, have grown stronger and smarter.

Further, New Jersey is part of a cultural shift that is changing politics in many northeastern areas as some high earners abandon traditional middle- and upper-class fiscally conservative values and vote liberal instead. In national elections, New Jersey today is now reliably in the "blue" column. The trend is also showing up in local elections, where longtime Republican strongholds like Millburn, Summit, and Madison have elected Democratic city councils and mayors for the first time. New Jersey may soon resemble its neighbor, New York City, as a place where the rich who tolerate high taxes or consider them a social obligation live side by side with the poor, but with a shrinking middle class.

In short, it may be that New Jersey, having for years enthusiastically welcomed New York's residents and jobs, is now watching the Empire State take a measure of revenge as its neighbor settles into a familiar high-tax, low-growth inertia. New Jersey has caught a bad case of the blue-state blues. We will discover in the next few years how permanent that case may be.

CHAPTER 4

We Don't Need Another War on Poverty

DO OUR CITIES need another War on Poverty? Barack Obama thinks so. Speaking before the U.S. Conference of Mayors in June 2008, the Democratic standard-bearer promised to boost spending on public schools, urban infrastructure, affordable housing, crime prevention, job training, and community organizing. The mayors, joined by many newspaper editorial pages, echoed Obama in calling for vast new federal spending on cities. All of this has helped rejuvenate the old argument that America's urban areas are victims of Washington's neglect and that it's up to the rest of the country (even though most Americans are now metro-dwellers) to bail them out.

Nothing could be more misguided than to renew this "tin-cup urbanism," as some have called it. Starting in the late 1960s, mayors in struggling cities extended their palms for hundreds of billions of federal dollars that accomplished little good and often worsened the problems they sought to fix. Beginning in the early nineties, however, a small group of reform-minded mayors—with New York's Rudy Giuliani and Milwaukee's John Norquist in the vanguard—jettisoned tin-cup urbanism and began developing their own bottom-up solutions to city problems. Their innovations made cities safer, put welfare recipients to work, and offered kids in failing school systems new choices, bringing about an incomplete, but very real, urban revival.

Yet this reform movement remains anathema to the big-government coalition of public-sector unions and social-service advocacy groups that consistently try to downplay its achievements because true reform entailed eliminating the very kinds of ineffective government programs that this coalition values. The arrival on the scene of Obama, a former Chicago community activist and the first president in recent memory to rise out of urban politics, gave these back-to-the-future voices their best chance in years to advance a liberal War on Poverty–style agenda. Still, it's crucial to remember what has worked to revive cities—and what hasn't.

The original War on Poverty, launched by the Johnson administration in the mid-sixties, was based on the assumption that Washington had to rescue American cities from precipitous—indeed, catastrophic—decline. It's important to remember that the cities themselves helped propel that decline. Political machines had long run the cities, and they imposed increasingly high taxes and throttling regulations on employers and often entrusted key government agencies, including police departments, to patronage appointees. The cities' industrial might protected them from serious downturns for a time. But as transportation advances beginning in the 1950s enabled businesses to relocate to less expensive suburbs or newer Sunbelt cities—and did so just as a generation of poor, uneducated blacks from the rural South began migrating to the urban North—the corrupt and inefficient machines proved unable to cope with the resulting economic and demographic shock. Urban poverty worsened (even as poverty was shrinking dramatically elsewhere); crime exploded; public schools, dominated by reform-resistant, inflexible teachers' unions, became incubators of failure, with staggering dropout rates for minority students; and middle-class city dwellers soon followed businesses out of town. Some industrial cities, scarred further by horrific race riots during the sixties, crumbled into near-ruins.

Yet the War on Poverty's legislative architects ignored the cities' own failings and instead embraced theories which argued that the external forces arrayed against the poor and cities, such as racism or globalization, were simply too overwhelming to address on the local level. "Officials and residents in urban communities are losing control of their cities to outside forces," warned urban planners Edward Kaitz and Herbert Harvey Hyman in their book *Urban Planning for Social Welfare*. "Cities are relatively powerless." The answer was federal intervention. Columbia University's Frances Fox Piven and Richard Cloward gained an influential following among policymakers by arguing that an unjust and racist nation owed massive government aid to the poor and mostly minority residents of struggling cities. Further, to compel those residents to work in exchange for help, or even to make them attend programs that might boost self-reliance, was to violate their civil liberties.

The War on Poverty, motivated by such toxic ideas, transformed welfare from temporary assistance into a lifelong stipend with few strings attached. As everyone knows, welfare rolls then skyrocketed, increasing 125 percent from 1965 to 1970 alone, and an entrenched generational underclass of poor families emerged. Typically they lived in dysfunctional public housing projects—many of them built as another battle in the War—that radiated blight to surrounding neighborhoods. The federal government created a series of huge initiatives, from Medicaid and Head Start to food stamps and school lunch programs, that spent billions of dollars trying to fight urban poverty. And then, to attack the "root causes" of poverty (whatever they were), the feds spent billions more on local social-services agencies, which ran ill-defined programs with vague goals like "community empowerment" that did nothing to alleviate poverty.

Despite years of effort and gargantuan transfusions of money, the federal government lost its War on Poverty. Poverty actually declined rapidly in America during the years before the Johnson administration rolled out its urban initiatives, tumbling from 22 percent in 1958 to 14 percent in 1967. Then, as Charles Murray observed in his unstinting examination of anti-poverty programs, *Losing Ground*, "Over the next twelve years, our expenditures on social welfare quadrupled. And in 1980, the percentage of poor Americans was—13 percent."

These programs did, however, produce a seismic shift in the way mayors viewed their cities—no longer as sources of dynamism and growth, as they had been for much of the nation's history, but instead as permanent, sickly wards of the federal government. In fact, as the problems of cities like Cleveland and New York festered and metastasized, mayors blamed the sickness on the federal government's failure to do even more. Norquist recalled a U.S. Conference of Mayors session held in the aftermath of the 1992 Los Angeles riots: "There was almost a feeling of glee among some mayors who attended: finally the federal government would realize it had to do something for cities."

Even as tin-cup urbanism prevailed, however, some mayors began arguing for a different approach, based on the belief that cities could master their own futures. The nineties became an era of fruitful urban-policy experimentation. For instance, well before the federal welfare reform of 1996, various cities and counties, most notably Giuliani's New York and Norquist's Milwaukee (encouraged strongly by Wisconsin governor Tommy Thompson), not only set limits on welfare eligibility for the programs they administered for the feds but also pursued a "work-first" policy that got able-bodied welfare recipients back into the workplace as swiftly as possible. Welfare rolls plummeted—in New York City, from 1.1 million in the early nineties to about 465,000 by 2001—and childhood poverty numbers decreased.

State and local legislators, often prodded by inner-city parents, also sought new ways to provide urban minority kids with a decent education. In Milwaukee a former welfare mother, enraged that her children had no option other than the terrible public schools, helped push a school-voucher bill through the Wisconsin state legislature, letting disadvantaged students use public money to attend private schools. Most states passed laws enabling private groups to set up charter schools unencumbered by many of the union-backed rules found in public school systems, such as restrictions on firing inferior teachers. Today some 4,300 charter schools, many in big cities, educate 1.2 million kids nationally—and most are performing, studies show, better than nearby public schools.

The era's most impressive urban reform improved public safety. Under Giuliani and his first police commissioner, William Bratton, New York City famously embraced Broken Windows policing, in which cops enforced long-dormant laws against public disorder, fostering a new climate of respect for the right of all citizens to use public spaces. The nineties' NYPD also introduced computer technology that tracked and mapped shifting crime patterns, so that police could respond quickly whenever and wherever crime spiked upward, and new accountability measures to ensure that commanders followed through. Crime in New York has plummeted 70 percent since the implementation of these reforms—double the national decline. Other cities that have adopted similar policing methods, from Newark to East Orange, New Jersey, to Raleigh, North Carolina, have had big crime turnarounds too. As Newark mayor Cory Booker, who tapped an NYPD veteran as police director, noted about crime-fighting: "There are models in America, right in New York City, that show that this is not an issue of *can* we, but *will* we."

President Obama may claim to be advancing a twenty-first-century agenda, but his ideas about aiding cities ignore the lessons of the nineties' reformers and remain firmly mired in the War on Poverty's vision of cities as victims who have been shortchanged by government. In education, for instance, though Obama has supported some education reforms such as charter schools, his plan for fixing urban schools emphasizes ever more money. In his signature education speech, Obama described visiting a high school outside Chicago that "couldn't afford to keep teachers for a full day, so school let out at 1:30 every afternoon," adding that "stories like this can be found across America." Later he said: "We cannot ask our teachers to perform the impossible, to teach poorly prepared children with inadequate resources."

In fact, the United States has made vast investments in its public schools. According to a study by Manhattan Institute scholar Jay Greene, per-student spending on K–12 public education in the United States rocketed from $2,345 in the mid-1950s to $8,745 in 2002 (both figures in 2002 dollars). Per-pupil spending in many cities is lavish. In New York, huge funding increases dating to the late 1990s have pushed per-pupil spending to $22,000; across the river in Newark, state and federal aid has boosted per-pupil expenditures to above $24,000; and Washington, D.C., now spends more than $22,000 a year per student. Yet these urban school systems have shown little or no improvement. "Schools are not inadequately funded—they would not perform substantially better if they had more money," Greene observes. An Organisation for Economic Co-operation and Development study found that most European countries spend between 55 percent and 70 percent of what the United States does per student, yet produce better educational outcomes. If some urban school systems are failing children, money has nothing to do with it.

President Obama also promises to invest heavily in the human capital of cities, seeking to forge a smarter, better-trained urban workforce. Yet here too his solutions look backward. His key proposal to help the chronically unemployable find work is simply to reauthorize the Workforce Investment Act of 1998. But politically connected insiders run many of the WIA's job-training initiatives, and waste is widespread. One Government Accountability Office study found that only about 40 percent of the $2.4 billion that the WIA designates for retraining dislocated workers actually went to the workers themselves; administrative costs gobbled up the rest. Even the money that reaches workers does little obvious good. In congressional testimony in 2007, a GAO official said, "We have little information at a national level about what the workforce investment system under WIA achieves."

Another big-ticket, War on Poverty–style item is to give cities more federal money to build "affordable" housing. Yet even as mayors warn about a critical shortage of housing for the poor and the middle class, many simultaneously claim they are hemorrhaging population because of competition from suburbs—and that should be lowering housing costs. Further, with foreclosures rising rapidly in some cities, cheap housing should be plentiful.

What explains this conundrum are the local policies that have helped make housing unaffordable. In a study called "The Planning Penalty," economist Randal O'Toole points out that half a century ago, when many cities were still gaining population, almost all of them boasted a healthy stock of affordable housing. Yet starting in the 1970s cities began aggressively limiting and directing housing growth, enacting rules for minimum lot sizes and population density that produced significant cost increases for builders, who passed them on to consumers. In Trenton, New Jersey, O'Toole estimates that the city-imposed planning penalty adds $49,000, or 17 percent, to the median cost of a home in a city where the population has shrunk from 130,000 in the 1950s to 85,000 today. In nearby Newark, a city pockmarked with empty lots that has lost some 170,000 residents, the planning penalty is $154,000, adding 41 percent to median home value. In New York, where Mayor Michael Bloomberg has committed $7.5 billion to build 165,000 units of affordable housing over ten years, the additional costs heaped on by government planning reach a whopping $311,000 per home. There's zero evidence that Obama understands the planning penalty at the heart of the affordable-housing shortage in many cities.

The U.S. Conference of Mayors also calls annually for an increase in HOPE VI funding as a way of getting welfare families to stop thinking of public housing as a permanent entitlement. The HOPE VI program, launched in the early nineties, got cities to replace large projects with smaller communities where the subsidized poor would live among those who could afford market-rate housing. The hope was that the bourgeois values of those earning their way in life would somehow rub off on the recipients of housing subsidies, who would then move up and out. But because the program imposed no actual requirements on the poor, the effort failed. Research has shown that in cities like Memphis, where the poor have been dispersed to middle-class neighborhoods, crime is rising.

Judging by these and other Obama initiatives, an urban-reform agenda based on the bottom-up successes of the 1990s still awaits its national advocate. It would start from the notion that cities can indeed be masters of their own futures. It would encourage city self-empowerment, not victimhood. Above all, it would urge municipalities to build on the stunning urban-policy successes of the 1990s.

The feds could still, however, play a useful role in several areas. One would be to help cities attack the chronic unemployment and lack of achievement among the urban poor, especially men recently released from prison with neither the schooling nor the workplace experience to find jobs. Nationwide some 700,000 prisoners finish their sentences every year. Lots go back to their home cities, where, aimless and unemployed, they reconnect with their old partners in crime, resume lawbreaking, and wind up back behind bars. Getting these former prisoners working might keep some from returning to crime; it could create a panoply of other benefits too, including allowing the many who are absentee fathers to begin supporting the children they left behind when they went to jail. Around the nation, one can find pockets of innovation on "prisoner reentry," often based on the same responsibility-building principles as welfare reform. Some of the most successful programs endorse a "work-first" philosophy that gets ex-cons back into the workplace under heavy supervision and mentoring rather than simply offering them job training. Promising demonstration projects have used local churches and community groups to run job-placement services, provide mentors to former prisoners, and then help them discover community resources.

Given the spectacular crime declines in New York and other cities that have followed its policing example, one might think that public safety is an area that requires no further federal role. But even as crime has begun rising again over the last few years in some cities, many police departments have shunned the new policing. Too many police officials and politicians continue to argue instead that factors beyond their control—from economic deprivation to cultural changes to bad federal policy—are to blame for crime. *Governing* magazine reports, for example, that Cleveland mayor Frank Jackson remains "skeptical about the ability of the police to solve the problem of crime, which he sees as deeply rooted in economic deprivation." Jackson told the magazine that "we look to the law, to the police, almost like an army that keeps everyone in check. That's a dangerous proposition." But a recent series of stories in the magazine *Cleveland Scene,* with titles like "The Killing Fields," reveals the consequences of such an attitude: a city under siege, with murders rising 56 percent from 2005 through 2007.

The federal government can help advance performance-based police work by aiding departments in implementing NYPD-style policing, including purchasing the necessary technology for crime mapping. The city of East Orange, for instance, used state grants and criminal forfeiture money to pay for its $1.5 million technology upgrade. Federal grants would be contingent on departments' demonstrating that they are practicing active—not reactive—policing, using the same measurements that innovative departments now use to judge their officers' productivity, such as the number of directed patrols aimed at preventing crimes, suspicious-activity stops, and field interrogations per officer.

The deplorable state of many city school systems puts education reform high on the list of any twenty-first-century urban-reform agenda. Here the Obama administration should be applauded for offering incentives for states and municipalities to increase the education choices offered to students, specifically to lift caps on charter schools. Today roughly half the states limit the number of charter schools they will authorize, one reason that about 365,000 students around the country remain on those schools' waiting lists. But state teachers' unions have vigorously fought against lifting these caps in places like New York and California, willing to forfeit hundreds of millions of dollars of federal aid.

The feds could also encourage schools to use curricula that work, especially to teach reading, since failing to learn to read in the early grades condemns many inner-city schoolchildren to fall permanently behind. The Bush administration admirably tried to prod school districts to adopt traditional, phonics-based programs, which are especially effective in educating minority students, the National Reading Panel concluded in 2000. But progressive educators who design curricula in local districts have continued to resist, favoring the ineffective but trendy "whole language" instruction touted by education schools.

As for increasing the amount of affordable housing, Washington could tie any housing aid to regulatory reforms that diminish or eliminate the construction caps and complex zoning requirements that drive up home prices. As Harvard economist Edward Glaeser has shown, some cities like Houston impose so few government costs on housing that quality housing gets built and sold at far lower prices than in more heavily regulated cities. Although Houston's economy boomed and its population grew by nearly one million during the 1990s, the price of housing there has increased at only slightly more than the rate of inflation.

At the same time the federal government should transform its policies on housing for the poor by employing the same philosophy that drove welfare reform, placing limits on tenure in public housing and requiring residents to work toward lifting themselves out of poverty. A few cities are, in fact, transforming public housing by ending the idea that everyone has a right to it and by imposing strict requirements on tenants. In the mid-nineties Atlanta began demolishing its giant projects, which once housed some fifty thousand poor residents, and replacing them with smaller mixed-income, mixed-use projects built with both federal money and large contributions from private developers who own and manage the housing. What attracted the private money was the promise from Atlanta's housing authority that these projects would be different: to live in them, all tenants between eighteen and sixty-five had to have jobs or be in school so that eventually they could graduate out of public housing entirely. Whereas in the mid-1990s fewer than 20 percent of the residents in Atlanta public housing were working, today it's about

70 percent. Federal housing authorities could adopt this model and urge other cities to follow it.

Obama's rise has put urban issues back into the national picture for the first time in decades. But the discussion about the future of America's cities continues to take place largely among politicians, commentators, and interest groups whose view of cities hasn't moved on much from the War on Poverty. We can't revisit the tin-cup urbanism that has kept so many cities in despair for so long. That's change we can do without.

CHAPTER 5

America's Worst Urban Program

IN 2005 the Bush administration proposed to eliminate one of the last and least effective vestiges of the War on Poverty: aid to cities doled out in the form of community-development block grants (CDBG). The president proposed slashing funding for this $5 billion-a-year boondoggle, which allows local officials virtually a free hand in spending federal money in their cities, and folding what remains of the block-grant program into other, more tightly focused and controlled grant schemes.

The effort failed, as have previous efforts to downsize or eliminate CDBG, even though over thirty years the program has expended some $100 billion in thousands of communities, with little to show for the effort. Local officials have squandered the billions by financing unworkable projects that often went bust, investing in new businesses that couldn't survive in depressed neighborhoods, and funding social programs with little idea of how they might actually strengthen their communities. A paradigmatic example of government ineffectiveness, this tempting pot of money gradually evolved into nothing more than a financer of ineffective and politically connected community groups, and a home of congressional pork spending. But precisely because of this the CDBG has powerful friends in Washington that blocked the Bush administration's efforts. The CDBG not only lives but President Obama, himself a product of government-funded community groups, has promised to vigorously expand it.

Created in response to the riots of the mid-1960s, urban-aid programs sprang from a belief of those radicalized years that the economic decline of inner cities resulted from external forces unconnected to the cities' own high-tax, anti-business policies or the growing culture of inner-city dependency, nurtured by a vast expansion of welfare. Instead such model-cities gurus as Edward M. Kaitz and Herbert Harvey Hyman, in their *Urban Planning for Social Welfare*, blamed urban decline on, among other things, federally subsidized home mortgages, which they argued encouraged the middle class to abandon the cities, and also on the nation's Protestant ethic, which directed private charitable institutions to target their aid only at the "worthy poor" who embraced our culture's values but skimped on aid to those who didn't. To counteract the sins of the federal government and of our bourgeois culture, federal officials proposed spending immense sums to rebuild neighborhoods, stimulate local economies, and finance social services that could restore the sense of community evaporating from inner-city neighborhoods as poverty demoralized their residents. President Johnson grandly asserted that with this investment the federal government would help create "cities of spacious beauty and living promise." The director of his Office of Economic Opportunity, Sargent Shriver, confidently predicted that the government could all but eliminate poverty in a decade. Buoyed by such optimistic self-assurance, Washington crafted a panoply of urban-aid programs and eventually rolled them into one gigantic block grant, funneling billions of dollars of urban aid to local public officials, many of whom understood little about the true causes of urban decline or about how the economies of cities and neighborhoods worked.

A graphic illustration of how little this money accomplished is the failure of the program's key initiative: a loan scheme designed to stimulate business in poor neighborhoods. War on Poverty planners had argued that poverty persisted in distressed areas partly because banks and other businesses redlined them, starving them of the investment they needed to revive by refusing to do business there. To counteract that lack of capital, the block-grant program poured hundreds of millions of dollars into businesses in poor communities, often financing companies that had difficulty repaying their debts, backing projects that went bust, and rarely creating jobs in the distressed areas at which they were targeted. Nationwide nearly 25 percent of block-grant-backed loans wind up in default, according to a recent analysis of dozens of community-lending portfolios. Even worse, a second HUD program—known as Section 108—which allows block-grant communities to raise money for loans by floating HUD-backed notes, had a staggering 59 percent default rate during Bush administration efforts to kill it.

When it comes to such lending programs, the bigger the effort, the worse the failure. In Los Angeles after the 1992 riots, for instance, the federal government plowed an astounding $430 million into a loan program designed to finance a cornucopia of jobs in east, south, and central Los Angeles but that went bust after creating pitifully few jobs. The federally sponsored Los Angeles Community Development Bank (LACDB) searched out worthy businesses in depressed areas, but since its crime-ridden target area remained an economically inhospitable place, the bank had trouble finding companies to lend to. Criticized for not making loans quickly enough, it then started pouring money unwisely into local businesses. It made one of its biggest loans to a former welfare recipient who had become a successful soft-drink salesman and wanted to open the country's first minority-owned dairy. The company racked up big losses, and, as the red ink spread, LACDB poured more money into the operation to keep it alive, until the bank had invested $24 million—violating its own lending limit. Even that wasn't enough to salvage the dairy, which closed only eighteen months after Vice President Al Gore touted it in a speech as a major success story of government-backed lending.

The dairy was far from LACDB's only failure. Just two years after the bank started making loans, nearly one-third of the companies in its portfolio had gone out of business or were delinquent in their payments—more than triple the default rate that the program had planned for. An HUD audit found that more than two-thirds of the 150 companies that received assistance did not create the required number of jobs in the enterprise zone where the bank operated, and that only 11 percent of the jobs generated went to the zone's residents, for whom they were intended. In 2009, in response to the audit, the Los Angeles City Council shut down the program, supposedly a national model for lending in troubled areas.

Like many CDBG programs, administration of the loan programs is rarely directed at ensuring that they actually accomplish what they are supposed to. An HUD audit found that in 30 percent of loans, local lending administrators didn't collect enough information to verify the job-growth objectives that were the very point of the program. And when the city auditor of Syracuse, a former private-sector banker, recently scrutinized the city's community-development loan program, he found not only that 60 percent of the loans were overdue; he was also stunned to learn that the program had no written lending criteria or standards for evaluating the viability of projects and companies, even though it had been pouring out money for years.

Urban aid can do little in cities whose own policies are hostile to real economic development, a key reason that the block-grant program has wasted so much money. Like Los Angeles, Buffalo has received huge infusions of federal urban aid—more than half a billion dollars in community-development block-grant money alone in thirty years. If this kind of urban aid truly worked, Buffalo would be a shining star in the economic-development constellation because it has gotten more block-grant money per capita than any other U.S. city. But as a series in the *Buffalo News* revealed, the city has almost nothing to show for its massive federal aid, having squandered it on a succession of failed projects. It poured nearly $60 million into trying to revive its theater district, with numerous loans and grants to private businesses that then defaulted, including hotels, restaurants, and arcades. Elsewhere in the city, government lent money to a developer to create a trade center near a Canadian border crossing, but it went bust. Various office-tower and hotel projects have also failed. More than $23 million of the nearly $38 million lent by the city through the Section 108 loan program alone has gone bad.

These projects failed because Buffalo offers little foundation for success, despite the boost from federal aid. The city, once a great manufacturing center, began to decline in the 1960s when, just as it was facing intense competition from other regions and from foreign goods, New York State officials began sharply raising taxes to pay for an expanding social agenda. The state also introduced new mandates, like requiring municipalities to pay a portion of the state Medicaid bill, which forced up property taxes too. First businesses, then residents began fleeing, and today Buffalo ranks as one of the nation's most depressed cities. The state and city have continued on this ruinous course. New York has, according to the Tax Foundation, the second-worst tax climate for businesses among the states; its workers' compensation system is the third most expensive for employers, nullifying Buffalo's continuing efforts to reinvigorate its industrial base. And despite fifty years of population loss, Buffalo has the highest state and local tax burden of any metropolitan area in the country.

A similar waste of federal money has occurred in cities around the country that were equally inhospitable to business and so squandered funds on doomed projects. For 20 years, starting in the mid-1970s, two blighted Baltimore neighborhoods—Park Heights and Upton—received some $100 million in federal aid, but by the mid-1990s they were "much worse off today than they were" at the start of the federal programs, according to an economic-development consultant who studied them. Over that time, in fact, Baltimore's economy shrank by 55,000 jobs while the city poured much of its block-grant money into recreational centers and street improvements that had little impact on the economy but were designed, according to a study by a local foundation, to placate community activists' demands for programs.

Conceived at a time when federal officials argued that communities should have wide latitude in deciding how to spend federal aid, the block-grant program has given local politicians a free hand in choosing what to invest in. Naturally they have pumped big sums into their favorite projects, many having nothing to do with revitalizing depressed neighborhoods. Too often these projects reflect what politicians believe the market *should* want, rather than what it really wants.

Governments, for instance, have used block grants to finance a building boom in convention centers and subsidized hotels that the private sector won't fund—a building boom that has yielded a nationwide glut of space, as cities have vied with one another for a largely flat business. Starting in the 1980s, cities of all sizes, from Washington, D.C., and Jacksonville, Florida, to St. Louis, Tulsa, and Orem, Utah, have used block-grant money to fuel this boom, despite mounting evidence that the business was becoming saturated. "While the supply of exhibit space in the United States has expanded steadily, the demand . . . has actually plummeted," according to a recent study by urban-planning expert Heywood Sanders of the University of Texas at San Antonio.

The building boom has sparked little, if any, economic development. The Washington, D.C., convention center, built with $834 million of public money, is attracting no more business than the city's previous, smaller center. Similarly, St. Louis's new Renaissance convention hotel, built with block-grant and other public money and touted as the final piece of a downtown renewal project, has been running at an occupancy rate below 50 percent, and rating agencies have put its government-backed bonds on credit watch.

Whatever economic development that block-grant money actually produces in a given locality almost always comes at the expense of somebody else, since communities now use federal urban aid to give businesses relocation incentives—in effect employing U.S. tax dollars to wage war against one another for existing jobs rather than creating new ones. Maryland, for instance, used block-grant money to buy land for a distribution center for Walmart, the world's largest company and one of its most profitable. Rhode Island and Delaware were also wooing the company to open the center on their turf. Similarly, Florida gave Sears, which Walmart replaced as America's largest retailer, a $5 million loan backed by community development block-grant money in order to keep the retailer from moving a distribution center to Georgia.

The early designers of urban-aid programs saw inner-city decay as more than just an economic matter. Poor neighborhoods were losing not only jobs but also their sense of community, advocates for the poor argued, and therefore, as the original block-grant legislation said, the government should help create "viable urban communities" by setting aside money for social services, from senior-citizen centers and youth sports leagues to mortgage-counseling services and AIDS-prevention efforts. But the notion of "community development" was so vague—if not downright specious—that it has been hard to measure the effectiveness of programs that fall under that rubric, and in most cases government stopped trying long ago. Billions of CDBG dollars have cascaded into social programs with little sense of how the money has been spent and whether it has helped achieve the program's original goal.

Occasional audits of these groups suggest that much of the money has gone to ineffective and inefficient programs, often run by politically connected operators. An analysis of Buffalo, for instance, which has spent about $75 million of CDBG money over the last three decades on social services, found that, over one three-year period, thirteen neighborhood housing groups helped initiate an average of only about two mortgages or home-repair loans per month each, nearly half of which were for $5,000 or less. Yet the groups collectively received about $1 million in annual funding and continued receiving it despite their poor performance.

If there are social services that demonstrably do good, municipalities have certainly not figured out how to target their block-grant spending to them in a way that achieves community-wide goals. After the 1992 riots in Los Angeles, for instance, Congress told the city and county that they could spend $14 million a year more on social programs aimed at "the underlying causes of the unrest"—as if everyone knew what they were. But the city and county just funneled the additional grant money largely into the existing array of senior centers, graffiti-removal programs, AIDS-prevention education, and so on. Little wonder that, according to a subsequent Government Accountability Office study, authorities could never "quantify how much public service funding was spent on the specific results or causes" of the riots, much less on whether that spending did anything to cure those problems. And little wonder that the federal Office of Management and Budget has criticized the entire block-grant program for lacking the means to measure the output or effectiveness of many of its grantees.

However wrong the War on Poverty planners turned out to be, they at least operated under the notion, misguided but sincere, that their programs might do some genuine good. But as time passed, local officials and Congress twisted the block-grant program for their own self-interested ends. They have allowed billions to go to politically connected groups, to congressional pork spending, and to wealthy communities—a far cry from the original intent of using the money to revive depressed neighborhoods.

Buffalo Common Council member Joseph Golombek, Jr., a critic of his city's block-grant efforts, calls local politicians "pigs feeding at the trough" of the program, and recent headlines from around the country make clear how widespread the problem is. In New London, Connecticut, for example, block-grant money funded an adult-education program run by the mayor's brother. In Yonkers, New York, the local chamber of commerce used a community-development block grant to run a program that employed a political ally of the mayor; when the mayor began feuding with the head of the chamber and withdrew the block grant, the chamber ended the program and fired the mayor's ally. In Buffalo a council member successfully sought block grants for a literacy program run by her son-in-law and for an AIDS-prevention organization that she founded and that employed her daughter. That's par for the course in Buffalo, where numerous developers and community groups receive block-grant funding, though their performance is never evaluated, says Golombek. "The people who run them and staff them write out checks for politicians and staff their campaigns," he says, "and they expect a payback."

In treating the program as a patronage tool, local officials are, of course, following the example of Congress. The less effective the program has turned out to be at reversing inner-city decline, the more congressmen have hijacked it for their own pork-barrel spending. Each year the HUD appropriations bill contains hundreds of member "earmarks," spending that is not part of the regular HUD grant-making process but instead is inserted by individual congressmen directly into federal legislation. These earmarks, totaling between $250 million and $300 million annually, have nothing to do with curing urban decay. An investigation by HUD's general counsel in the late 1980s disclosed that members of Congress were using the program for such pet projects as sugarcane mills in Hawaii and a recreation center on Mackinac Island, a tiny Michigan resort boasting a Grand Hotel and restored Victorian homes—about as far from urban decay as one can get in America.

A few years later President Clinton's transition team issued a blistering report that warned of the "systematic plunder of many millions of taxpayer dollars" in block grants and other HUD programs. It hasn't stopped: in the last several years congressmen have lavished over $2 million in grants on zoos, $340,000 for opera houses in Connecticut, Michigan, and Washington State, money for the Southern New Mexico Fair and Rodeo, the Alabama Quail Trail, and the Iao Theater in Wailuku, Hawaii. In election years the block-grant program becomes a particularly valuable political piñata. In the 2002 elections, for instance, U.S. Senate Democrats, trying to protect their slim majority, inserted $31 million in block-grant earmarks into HUD legislation for states with close races—a 50 percent increase over the previous year in those states.

Little wonder, then, that politicians like New York's Senator Charles Schumer ignore the manifold failings of the program, amply detailed in studies by everyone from the GAO to the HUD Office of Inspector General, and insist that block grants are the "seed corn for urban development and job growth" and "the single most important tool that cities like New York have to grow"—statements so at odds with the facts that they are simply ludicrous.

One of the most corrosive consequences of the War on Poverty is that it created an entitlement culture that soon spread to politicians from poor neighborhoods to pols representing the wealthy and the middle class too. This entitlement mentality has thoroughly infected the block-grant program. Soon after it began, mayors of thriving cities and congressional representatives from posh districts began complaining about their exclusion from the program. To win their support, the Carter administration expanded urban aid to include "non-distressed" communities. As a result, thousands of municipalities free of urban blight have used federal money to build tennis courts in tennis-playing neighborhoods, to finance arts centers, or to pretty up their downtown shopping districts. The town of Parkland, Florida, where family income is more than twice the national average, has used block-grant money to spiff up its local community center. Bergen County, New Jersey, where annual household income is 55 percent above the national average, spent nearly $280,000 in block-grant money over a three-year period to keep alive a privately owned local theater and arts center less than half an hour from Broadway. The town of Lower Merion, Pennsylvania, where household income is more than double the national average, has spent some of its block-grant money to compile a history of a local train station.

Some wealthy cities, like Greenwich, Connecticut, and Newton, Massachusetts, defend the program by pointing out that they too have lower-income residents and that their programs focus on these few. But the original legislation aimed to provide federal aid not to poor people everywhere but to the poor in cash-strapped cities whose budgets were under strain. By contrast, these wealthy communities have enormous tax bases and robust city budgets that could pay for services to the poor without help from the feds. Greenwich's tax base is so healthy, for instance, that the town's school system spends about $18,000 per pupil annually—about twice the national average—yet Washington is contributing hundreds of thousands of dollars a year to finance social programs there. Similarly, when state aid to cities declined in Massachusetts during the last recession, residents of Newton simply voted to raise their taxes by $11 million rather than cut any services. But taxpayers across the country are paying for the wealthy town's block-grant programs. "Block grants have helped spur a redistribution of income from moderate communities to some privileged rich ones," says National Taxpayers Union vice president Pete Sepp.

Given the awful track record of this program, the Bush Office of Management and Budget recommended excising billions that now go to well-off neighborhoods, and vastly reducing spending on social-services programs. The administration wanted to give what would be left of the block-grant program to the Commerce Department and focus it on one purpose only—helping to boost distressed neighborhoods. And considering how poorly even these efforts have often turned out, the Office of Management and Budget demanded that projects receiving funds demonstrate their effectiveness using such traditional measures as increases in jobs, gains in property values, or declines in neighborhood crime. Cities would have to compete with one another to win such aid, rather than receiving funds each year based on a preordained formula.

The administration lost its battle, however, because everyone from congressmen in wealthy districts to urban politicians defends CDBG. Over the years this coalition has saved the program and resisted even modest changes, because its supporters view it as entitlement—free money to plug their budget deficits and finance city-employee salaries. New York, for instance, uses a portion of its block grant to pay the salaries of city building inspectors and lawyers in its housing department. Buffalo has spent some $100 million of its block-grant money over 30 years on government salaries, at one point paying some 230 city hall workers through the program. The potential of losing that windfall prompted hyperventilation from local pols, perhaps none sillier than the response of former Baltimore mayor Martin O'Malley, who compared the Bush administration's proposed block-grant cuts to terrorist attacks on our nation's "core cities."

The CDBG lives for another day, and President Obama promises to increase its size. Considering the country's huge, $1.5 trillion debt in fiscal year 2010, the program is a tiny part of our national budgetary problems. But something larger is at stake. For thirty years critics have been unable to reform or eliminate a program that is ineffective at best, with no clear goals, and a clear patronage machine for politicians and community groups at worst, with a long series of scandals behind it. The persistence of CDBG exemplifies how difficult reform becomes once a government program becomes entrenched.

CHAPTER 6

The Movement to Undermine Welfare Reforms

IN SOCIAL-SERVICES JARGON, Debra Autry had "multiple barriers to work" when the State of Ohio told her that she had to start earning her welfare benefits. Autry had been out of work and on public assistance for more than two decades, and she lacked many of the skills necessary for a modern economy. She was a single mother too, like most welfare recipients, with three kids at home. Autry was skeptical about working in the private sector, so the state placed her in a publicly subsidized program that had her cleaning government offices in exchange for her benefits. Disliking the work, Autry landed a cashier's job at a local Revco drugstore, arranging her hours around her children's school day. After the CVS chain bought out Revco, she enrolled in the company's program to learn how to become a pharmacy technician and eventually began working in that position, which typically pays between

$25 and $30 per hour. "I was on welfare because there were no jobs that interested me," she recalls. "But once I had to go back to work, I realized there's a future if you want to better yourself. It was the best decision I ever made."

Autry's story is the kind that reformers dreamed about back in 1996, when President Bill Clinton signed the federal Personal Responsibility and Work Opportunity Reconciliation Act, often referred to as the welfare reform act. That legislation, drawing on earlier innovations in Wisconsin and New York City, put time limits on aid and required some recipients to work in order to end the culture of long-term dependency that no-strings-attached public assistance had helped foster. Autry's success story turned out to be one of many. Since 1996, welfare caseloads have plummeted by 70 percent—8.8 million people off the rolls, which today are down to 3.8 million.

In fact, during the first few years of welfare reform, the rolls fell so quickly that many state welfare agencies, which administer welfare for the federal government, stopped feeling pressure to move their remaining welfare clients back into the workforce. That prompted a movement to further stiffen welfare reform, enacted in 2005, which required states to put even more people back to work.

And yet, despite the enormous success of welfare reform, it remains constantly under attack and in danger of being watered down every time it must be reauthorized. Prodded by social-services advocates who design and run many of the community programs that welfare reform stopped funding, and urged on by state welfare bureaucrats pressured by reform to meet strict federal standards, some in Congress have pledged to roll back the original reforms and make it easier for people to stay on public assistance for longer periods without work. Although it's clear after more than a decade that the new welfare regime is far more successful at lifting people out of poverty than the old program, which encouraged lifelong dependency, it's also evident that the case for sustaining welfare reform will have to be made over and over again.

The 1996 welfare legislation gave states enormous flexibility in fulfilling its requirements, and many interpreted the law liberally. Although recipients were required to work, some states counted as "work" the hours that recipients spent in treatment for alcohol or drug addiction or in traveling to and from job-training sessions. Others let recipients satisfy work obligations by "helping a friend or relative with household tasks or errands," according to a 2005 Government Accountability Office study. Certain states allowed home exercise, "motivational reading," and anti-smoking classes to qualify recipients for aid, reasoning that such practices could at least lead to work.

Despite such laxity, four million welfare recipients left the rolls during the first two years after President Clinton signed the reform into law. Since many states previously had required virtually nothing of welfare clients, simply compelling them to meet with caseworkers to discuss work options was enough to propel many out the door to look for jobs. "Everyone underestimated the ability of single mothers to go back to work," says Grant Collins, former deputy director of the Office of Family Assistance in the Department of Health and Human Services (HHS).

The number of leavers was so big, in fact, that it all but eliminated many states' federal requirements to keep moving people off welfare. The legislation required states' work-participation rates—that is, the percentage of people on welfare who were working or searching for work—to be at least 50 percent. But states were allowed to diminish that fraction by whatever percentage their welfare rolls had shrunk since 1995. By 2002 welfare rolls nationwide had fallen so steeply that thirty-three states could meet their obligations with work-participation rates of less than 10 percent.

That undesirable situation led to a three-year battle to reauthorize and reenergize welfare reform. The result was the 2005 Budget Reconciliation Act, which changed the year from which states could calculate case reductions from 1995 to 2005, thereby ending the generous credit that most states enjoyed from their huge initial drop in welfare cases. Between 40 and 50 percent of states' adult welfare recipients now had to go back to work, search for a job, or otherwise prepare to work. The federal government also tightened the definition of what counts in fulfilling the work requirement: no longer would spending time in psychological counseling or in traveling to job training do the trick. And the feds urged states to enroll more welfare recipients with physical or mental disabilities in job-training and job-placement programs. "Individuals who happen to have disabilities should be afforded the same opportunities to engage in work—to find work-related training, work experience, and employment—as those who do not have a disability," the Bush administration's Department of Health and Human Services wrote in its new regulations.

Advocates and some pols charged that many of those remaining on welfare were too troubled for states to hit the demanding new work-participation targets. Urban League president Marc Morial complained that the bill would "subject families to harsher work requirements with inadequate funding" for social services to help them adjust. He scored the bill in particular for limiting how long someone could remain on welfare while pursuing a college degree. "We don't have many families left. Those remaining have multiple issues," objected the head of Welfare Advocates, a Maryland-based coalition of social-services agencies and churches. A 2002 Urban Institute finding that 44 percent of welfare recipients faced two or more "barriers to work" became a frequent citation.

HHS basically discounted such complaints in writing its new welfare regulations, in part because the critics were defining "barrier to work" too loosely. The Urban Institute study, for instance, considered the lack of a high school diploma, being out of the workforce for three or more years, or lack of English proficiency as obstacles to work, while other groups argued that being a single parent was a major barrier. A common demand was that welfare programs first provide day-care services for single parents or treatment for addicts before requiring any work. "I was at a White House conference in the mid-1990s in which someone observed that we couldn't require single mothers on welfare to go back to work until we had day care for all of them," recalls Peter Cove, co-founder of America Works, an employment service for welfare recipients. "I stood up and said that if we tried to solve every problem before asking people to work, we'd never get any recipient back in the workforce."

The 2005 bill wholly embraced this "work-first" philosophy. Work-first originally emerged as a welfare reform model in the 1980s, adopted by Wisconsin governor Tommy Thompson; in the mid-nineties Mayor Rudy Giuliani enthusiastically signed on in New York City. At its core, work-first maintains that the biggest obstacle to employment many welfare clients face is their own lack of understanding of the fundamentals of any workplace—showing up for work regularly and on time, for instance. The best way to help such people isn't to put them in elaborate job-training programs, this approach holds, but simply to get them working—even in entry-level positions—under the careful supervision of a caseworker, who makes sure they get up in the morning and out the door. Caseworkers will even help out with recipients' child-care emergencies or get alcoholic clients to continue in treatment—but all with the aim of keeping them on the job. "Many of the best therapeutic programs for people with problems like alcoholism don't think it's a good idea for people to stop working and go home and sit on a couch all day after counseling," says Tom Steinhauser, head of Virginia's welfare division. "Why should welfare programs treat people any different?"

A work-first approach has helped sustain deep reductions in New York City's welfare population, long after rolls stopped dropping in some states. By the time Rudy Giuliani left office in 2001, the city's welfare numbers had fallen from 1.1 million to 475,000, and they're down another 25 percent, to 330,000, under Mayor Michael Bloomberg, who has continued the reforms. Many of those who wind up on welfare today remain "work-ready," argues Robert Doar, commissioner of Gotham's Human Resources Administration (HRA), which is why the city has been able to place some 70,000 to 80,000 of them a year in jobs.

The "work-ready" population is evident at the crowded Manhattan offices of America Works, where I went to observe co-founder Lee Bowes address a new group enrolled in the organization's counseling and employment program. Every seat is taken, and even the windowsills are occupied. When one attendee asks why the classroom is so crowded, Bowes bluntly responds: It's because lots of people are looking for jobs. Asked by Bowes how she wound up on welfare, a single mother explains that her apartment building burned and that she and her children found themselves temporarily homeless. She then lost her job and went on public assistance; she says that she's ready, though, to get back to work. Is this the first agency she has visited since going on welfare? Bowes wonders. The woman's answer elicits nods from the group: "I went somewhere where they treated me like I was in kindergarten. They asked me if I was ready to go back to work. I said yes—can you help me find a job? Then I heard that this place does that. So I'm here now."

Most of these welfare recipients will wind up in entry-level jobs. The average starting wage for someone coming off welfare in New York is slightly above $9 an hour, according to the HRA. But with other assistance, like the federal and state earned income tax credits, food stamps, and Medicaid, a recipient's actual annual income can rise well above $20,000—not enough for an extravagant lifestyle in

New York, of course, but enough to allow her to get back on her feet and start down the road to independence. This aid menu is typical across the country, even if assistance levels vary. With the decline in welfare rolls, states now spend more on noncash assistance programs, like food stamps, than on welfare itself.

Many employers have tapped this labor pool because it has been hard for them to fill entry-level positions. New York City–sponsored job fairs for welfare recipients attract dozens of companies. America Works says that it has a reliable list of employers ready to hire welfare recipients for entry-level jobs. Even in an economic downturn, like the 2008–2009 recession or the national recession that began in mid-2001, employers keep seeking entry-level workers because of the high turnover rate for these jobs. Welfare rolls didn't rise in New York City during the last recession, it's worth noting.

One of those eager entry-level employers is CVS, which has hired about 63,000 people off welfare nationwide over the last decade or so. Some 60 percent still work for the chain, an extraordinary statistic for an industry with high turnover. The typical former welfare recipient at CVS has had at least two promotions. Some, like Autry, have gone through training in CVS's pharmacy technician program; others have returned to school with the chain's help and earned pharmacist's degrees. One key to their success with former welfare recipients, CVS has learned, is to work closely with state agencies and their contractors, who'll lend a hand with the new hires for several months or longer to ease their transition to employment. "We learned early on that you just don't throw someone into a full-time job right away without some support," says Steve Wing, director of workforce initiatives at CVS. "We rely on the agencies to help these people adjust."

Many state agencies and advocacy groups have derided entry-level jobs in retailing or in service industries—the places where welfare recipients will most likely find work—as pointless, "dead-end" employment. It was this foolish and hoary objection, dating back to the welfare debates of the seventies, that for years thwarted efforts to get welfare recipients working. "We heard the line about dead-end jobs so often from people running welfare agencies that we drew up a poster showing the career opportunities for people at CVS who start by working as cashiers in stores," says Wing. "The stores are where a lot of our managerial employees start, but there's just a perception among those who run welfare programs that these entry-level jobs are not good enough."

Under the revised welfare rules, however, states can no longer ignore such employers and their jobs, and more states are reshaping their programs along work-first lines. Over the last two years, for instance, seventeen states have created more stringent contracts for local private agencies working with welfare recipients, requiring them to meet job-placement targets or risk penalties. Arizona has told its contractors that if the federal government penalizes the state for failing to meet work goals, the contractors must share in the punishment. Private groups must even prove when bidding for Arizona contracts that they have sufficient financial reserves to pay any fines. But the state will also give bonuses to agencies that perform job placement well.

Several states have imposed stricter standards even on their own public agencies. In California, new legislation lets the state pass on to county welfare offices any financial penalties that it might incur for failing to meet the new federal regulations. County administrators also must file plans explaining how they intend to meet their new requirements, and county work-participation rates now get shared throughout the system, so everyone can see how each county is performing. Pennsylvania, which had a dismal 7 percent work-participation rate for its approximately forty thousand adult welfare recipients in 2005, not only has started grading each county program but publishes the entire list online.

States are also requiring welfare applicants to begin job searches or undergo employment counseling much more quickly than in the past. Eleven states have altered application procedures to include some kind of employment assessment for people when they first request welfare. New applicants in Delaware, for instance, must spend two weeks working with an employment and training counselor before receiving benefits. Missouri no longer considers a welfare application complete unless the applicant has met with an employment counselor and worked out a job-search plan.

In many states welfare recipients once could keep getting benefits even when they refused to comply with work or vocational requirements, an enormous impediment to reform. Since the 2005 legislation, however, ten states that previously only partially reduced a welfare recipient's check for failing to participate in such programs have now moved to "full sanctions," that is, cutting off benefits completely. Other states, while not going as far, have implemented harsher penalties or are at least considering doing so.

Welfare programs are also launching more joint private-public training ventures, aimed at funneling recipients directly into jobs. Welfare and employment agencies in Atlanta, Baltimore, Cleveland, Detroit, and Washington, D.C., have tapped CVS, because of its previous experience hiring former welfare clients, to establish training centers—essentially, replicas of its stores—where recipients can prepare for full-time jobs at the chain. Hawaii has formed a similar partnership with local banks, resulting in more than three hundred welfare recipients' getting placed in permanent jobs. New York City has joined with cable TV and phone companies to train welfare recipients as customer-service representatives.

Agencies are also taking a harder look at programs that try to get those who claim to have physical or mental barriers to work on the path toward employment. Sometimes this means encouraging them to begin part-time work or to undergo counseling to see what kind of training and work they might qualify for. "States are doing things that sound really simple, like having their own doctors assess those who claim they can't work," says Jason Turner, who designed Wisconsin's welfare-to-work programs and is now a Milwaukee-based consultant. "But you would be surprised how many states were merely accepting notes from a welfare recipient's doctor, excusing them from work."

One model is WeCare, which handles New York City's toughest cases. Welfare recipients who say they can't work are enrolled in this program, in which a city-employed doctor and a caseworker evaluate them. If the doctor decides that a person can work but has a condition—a bad back or asthma, say—that restricts the types of jobs he can do, the caseworker draws up a job-search plan based on those limitations. Welfare recipients not well enough to work immediately but not permanently disabled are put on a treatment regimen to get them healthier and employable. "If they are exempt from work, they must still participate in treatments and in vocational rehabilitation programs," says Michael Bosket, who heads WeCare. "Everyone does something."

Typically, about 6 percent of the recipients referred to WeCare are deemed employable and sent directly back to a caseworker to find a job; another 43 percent are found employable with limitations. "Many people who used to be considered having barriers to work really have barriers to certain kinds of jobs, but they shouldn't be exempt from work," says Cove. Of the nearly 24,000 people in the WeCare program in the fall of 2008, about 3,000 worked or enrolled in approved work-participation programs, about 7,000 were undergoing treatment or vocational therapy, and some 8,500 had been judged permanently disabled by the city's doctors and directed to apply for federal disability benefits, which are separate from the welfare system. (The rest of the WeCare group was still undergoing evaluation.)

Despite these successes, the system remains under criticism. President Obama, for instance, turned down several opportunities during the 2008 campaign to say whether he would have signed the welfare reform act if he had been president in 1996; he preferred not to look back, he said, but forward. During the campaign he did run ads crediting the 1997 Illinois law that he helped write—which brought the state's welfare system in line with federal changes—with Illinois' decline in welfare caseloads.

Congress's most powerful Democratic leaders have also opposed welfare reform. Speaker of the House Nancy Pelosi voted against both the 1996 legislation (calling it "punitive and unrealistic") and the 2005 bill. Harry Reid, the Senate majority leader, used language strikingly similar to that of social-services advocates to criticize welfare reform. On its tenth anniversary he declared that "many welfare recipients face significant barriers to employment" and that states need "flexibility" in aiding them.

What the advocates hope to gain from critics of welfare reform would be an effort to unwind some key elements of the law, such as the restrictions on counting certain kinds of job training or substance-abuse counseling as work. Such moves would almost certainly inflate work-participation rates artificially and blunt some of the effectiveness of the reforms. And it is even possible that a future Congress would attempt to go further, digging into the original 1996 legislation and curtailing some of its mandates. As the Manhattan Institute's Heather Mac Donald has warned, "Powerful political forces" have not stopped "trying to make dependency acceptable again."

CHAPTER 7

The Religious Left, Reborn

EVERYONE KNOWS that the Christian Right is a potent force in American politics. But since the mid-nineties an increasingly influential religious movement has arisen on the left, mostly escaping the national press's notice. The movement expends its political energies not on the cultural concerns that primarily motivate conservative evangelicals but instead on an array of labor and economic issues. Working mostly at the state and local level, and often in lockstep with unions and social advocacy groups, the ministers, priests, rabbis, and laity of this new Religious Left have lent their moral authority to a variety of left-wing causes, exerting a major, sometimes decisive influence in campaigns to enforce a "living wage," to help unions organize, and to block the expansion of nonunionized businesses like Walmart, among other struggles. Indeed, the movement's effectiveness has made it one of organized labor's most reliable allies.

The new Religious Left is in one sense not new at all. It draws its inspiration from the Christian social-justice movement that formed in the mid-nineteenth century as a response to the emerging industrial economy, which many religious leaders viewed—with some justification—as brutal and unfair to workers. In America the movement gained traction thanks largely to the efforts of the Baptist minister Walter Rauschenbusch, who served New York City's poor. Unlike nineteenth-century reformers who sought to help the poor by teaching them the bourgeois virtues of hard work, thrift, and diligence, Rauschenbusch believed that the best way to uplift the downtrodden was to redistribute society's wealth and forge an egalitarian society. In Christ's name, capitalism had to fall. "The Kingdom of God is a collective conception," Rauschenbusch wrote in *Christianity and the Social Crisis*, politicizing the Gospel's message. "It is not a matter of getting individuals to heaven, but of transforming the life on earth into the harmony of heaven."

Rauschenbusch's "social gospel," as it came to be called, fell out of favor after World War I, when the violence of the Russian Revolution and the radicalization of European workers alarmed many American Christians. But in milder forms the notion persisted that clergy should minister to the needy not by guiding souls to heavenly paradise but by seeking structural changes in society. In 1919 the Catholic philosopher Monsignor John Ryan gained a wide following by calling for pro-union legislation, steep taxes on wealth, and more stringent business regulation. When Franklin Roosevelt adopted several of Father Ryan's ideas in the 1930s, the priest was given the sobriquet the "Right Reverend New Dealer." His popularity reflected the tightening alliance between America's mainstream churches and organized labor.

That alliance disintegrated during the 1960s. Left-wing clerics like the rebel priests the Berrigan brothers began to agitate for a wider range of radical causes—above all, a swift end to the Vietnam War. The more culturally conservative blue-collar workers who formed the union movement's core wanted no part of this. The rift between the Religious Left and labor leaders would last for several decades.

The mending of that rift—and the arrival on the political scene of a new, union-friendly, Religious Left during the mid-nineties—owes much to the tireless efforts of savvy labor bosses, especially AFL-CIO president John Sweeney. The son of Irish immigrants, Sweeney grew up in a prototypical Catholic pro-union household; when he took over the AFL-CIO in 1996, he resolved to restore the bonds between church and labor. In a 1996 speech to a Catholic symposium, Sweeney evoked an era when labor unions were mighty and churches stood squarely behind them: "In our modest home in the Bronx, there were three things central to our lives: our family, the Church, and the union," he recalled. With union membership shrinking—from 24 percent of the workforce thirty years ago to 14.5 percent in 1996 (and just 11 percent today)—"unions need aggressive participation by the Church in our organizing campaigns," he implored church leaders.

The Sweeney-led AFL-CIO reenergized the old alliance. Soon after he took office, the AFL-CIO launched "Labor in the Pulpits," a program that encouraged churches and synagogues to invite union leaders to preach the virtues of organized labor and tout its political agenda.

Labor in the Pulpits has steadily expanded: nearly a thousand congregations in one hundred cities nationwide now take part annually. Sweeney himself has preached from the pulpit of Washington, D.C.'s National Cathedral, urging congregants to join anti-globalization protests in the capital. In Los Angeles, caravans of union activists have visited black churches on Labor Day Sunday, dispensing contributions from union locals. San Jose union leaders, seeing amnesty for illegal aliens as a way to garner new recruits, have asked churchgoers to support it. And in Des Moines, a vice president of the United Steelworkers told a Methodist congregation: "In America today, the pursuit of profits takes precedence over the pursuit of justice—and working families are suffering the consequences."

Under the auspices of Labor in the Pulpits, clerics in America's mainstream churches—Catholics, Lutherans, Methodists, and Presbyterians—have composed guidelines for union-friendly sermons and litanies as well as inserts for church bulletins that promote union legislation. One insert, distributed in 2006, asked congregants to pray for a federal minimum-wage hike and also—if the prayers didn't work, presumably—to contact their congressional representatives. Another recent one encouraged churchgoers to arrange home viewings of an anti-Walmart documentary, to stop shopping at the retail giant, and to patronize Costco, a unionized competitor. A 2005 insert urged congregants to lobby Congress to pass the Employee Free Choice Act—controversial legislation that would let unions organize firms merely by getting workers to sign authorizing cards rather than by conducting secret ballots, as is currently required.

Unions are also cultivating the next generation of church leaders. "Seminary Summer," an initiative created with the Chicago-based, union-supported Interfaith Worker Justice (IWJ), arranges for seminarians to spend the summer months working with union locals. "Within three years most of these students will be in leadership positions in congregations," predicted IWJ head Kim Bobo shortly after the program began in 2000. Since then, some two hundred seminarians have helped unionize Mississippi poultry workers, aided the Service Employees International Union in organizing Georgia public-sector employees, and bolstered campaigns for living-wage legislation in California municipalities.

Seminary Summer seems to be sparking considerable enthusiasm among participants. "Before Seminary Summer, I had been leery, even suspicious, of labor unions," remarked Lori Peterson of Loyola University, a 2006 enrollee. But afterward, she said, "I began to believe in the labor movement again. The training gave me a new perspective on unions and how important they are to creating equality and justice." Chicago Divinity School student Beau Underwood, who took part in 2007, is equally fervent. "One staple of a union organizer's toolbox is the bullhorn and I love it," he noted on his blog. "One of the very first days I led chants during an early-morning hotel picket line. Just today, I 'bullhorned' at customers of a hotel being boycotted by the union."

"Younger seminarians may be particularly receptive to such experiences," suggests Father Robert Sirico of the Acton Institute, which tries to educate religious leaders on the compatibility of free-market principles with Christian beliefs. "Seminarians are preaching all the time," he adds, "and if they don't have an economic background, it's easy for them to fall into the fallacy of the Left that our economy is a zero-sum game that demands conflict between business owners and workers."

Working with IWJ, the labor movement has spawned some sixty new Religious Left groups, ranging from the Massachusetts Interfaith Committee for Worker Justice to the Chicago Interfaith Committee on Worker Issues to the Los Angeles–based Clergy and Laity United for Economic Justice (Clue). These organizations have given unions an effective ally, especially in town councils, city halls, and state capitols, which have proven more union-friendly than Washington, D.C., in recent years.

Nowhere have these efforts borne more fruit than in Los Angeles, where Clue has recruited some six hundred religious leaders to back worker causes. Clue clergy helped crush several 2005 California ballot initiatives that unions opposed, including one that gave public sector union workers the option of not paying dues that would fund union political activities. In 2006 Clue pressure, including a fast for striking workers, helped prompt building owners in greater L.A. to allow security guards to unionize. Two years earlier Clue had united about fifty local congregations to support four thousand workers demanding more money and better benefits from seventeen area hotels. Clergy asked the faithful to boycott the hotels until their owners caved—as, in the end, they did.

Interfaith coalitions have scored similar victories elsewhere. In Memphis, for instance, clergy fought relentlessly—via newspaper op-eds, public fasts, and preaching—

for the passage of living-wage bills that since 2004 have forced local businesses to hike wages well above the federal minimum. "The living-wage effort here was pushed mainly by local clergy," says Ken Hall, former vice president for the Memphis Regional Chamber of Commerce, which battled the measures.

Noting the success of Memphis's living-wage battle and of similar campaigns in which religious leaders have played key roles, unions and their allies have made recruiting Religious Left support part of the activist playbook—an inspired strategy, since polls show that even secular Americans consider clergy our most admired profession. The Wayne State University Labor Studies Center's "activist handbook" advises living-wage campaigns always to put religious leaders out front. "As soon as you have clergy arguing for something called a 'living wage,' you've lost the battle if you're representing businesses," Hall observes. "If I was debating against union members advocating for a 'surplus wage law,' which is what living-wage laws actually are, we would have won." Pro-labor Berkeley city councilman Kriss Worthington echoes the point from the other side of the fence. "When a politician or union proposes something, people start out with a questioning attitude," he said after clerics helped sway the council to endorse a labor initiative. "When you have a faith community, it adds a moral and ethical component"—all the more effective in that the Religious Left essentially has the spiritual terrain to itself on economic matters, which Christian conservative groups have mostly ignored. The labor-religious coalitions have worked spectacularly well: some 125 municipalities have passed living-wage laws.

Some of America's most venerable Protestant denominations have thrown their institutional weight behind the new alliance with labor. More than a hundred religious organizations support IWJ financially, including the National Council of Churches of the U.S.A. (NCC), an umbrella organization of nearly forty mainstream Christian denominations. Key NCC members such as the Presbyterian Church (U.S.A.), the Evangelical Lutheran Church in America, and the Episcopal church are particularly active. Though it was founded in 1950 to promote ecumenical cooperation, the NCC has become a clearinghouse for religious participation in left-wing causes. Heavily funded by liberal groups like the Tides Foundation and the Ford Foundation, during the 2004 national elections the NCC organized the Let Justice Roll campaign, which focused on voter registration drives in Democratic areas, and it renewed the campaign in 2006, this time with an emphasis on helping statewide groups pass referenda raising the minimum wage.

The new alliance between labor and religion also enjoys the powerful backing of the Catholic church, whose American hierarchy, though often conservative on social issues, is firmly left wing in its economic views. Several dozen major Catholic groups—including the Catholic Conference of Bishops, Catholic Charities, and the Archdiocese of Los Angeles—contribute financially to interfaith workers' groups and assist their lobbying efforts. At a national conference, Bishop Gabino Zavala of Los Angeles went so far as to compare labor leaders with Old Testament prophets, praising them for "bringing the same conviction, ideals, passion, commitment to justice, energy for human rights, and sense of mission to their bold words and actions, to their union organizing and coalition building."

Having established itself in many places as the moral authority on economic issues, the resurgent Religious Left has brought back the fiery redistributionist language of the social gospel. Clerical anti-capitalism increasingly echoes Rauschenbusch's old notion that "it is hard to get riches with justice." In a scriptural reflection distributed for Labor in the Pulpits, the Reverend Darren Wood, a Methodist and the author of *Blue Collar Jesus*, declared that Christ envisioned "an alternate economy of equality." To achieve that egalitarian vision, the IWJ's Bobo pronounced, America needs a "redistribution" to "shift wealth from a few to working families."

The Religious Left reserves some of its most hyperbolic rhetoric for Walmart, the labor movement's bête noire. Clergy describe the giant retailer in terms that its thousands of suppliers, millions of employees, and tens of millions of customers would hardly recognize. The Reverend Jarvis Johnson, an IWJ board member, has urged congregants to invite the "hurting, blind and crippled" to a metaphorical banquet. Who are these poor, abused souls? "They are Walmart associates who have to wait six months to a year to qualify for a health-care plan," Johnson explained. The Reverend Alexia Salvatierra, a Lutheran minister and head of Clue, compares Walmart with "the noblemen of Luther's time," whom the German monk denounced for robbing the poor.

Religious Left leaders have blindly accepted all that the unions claim about corporate America's sins. In backing the Employee Free Choice Act, for instance, clerics argue that laws and rulings by anti-union government bureaucrats have crippled workers' ability to organize—the big reason, they claim, that union membership has plummeted. "Our government seems determined to undermine the people's right to organize in the United States," charged the Reverend Nelson Johnson, in reaction to a National Labor Relations Board ruling that broadened the definition of "supervisor," narrowing the number of people eligible to join unions as hourly employees. Such explanations ignore the real reason for labor's decline. A 2005 Zogby poll found that only 35 percent of nonorganized workers would join a union if given the opportunity. And contrary to the clerics who rail against corporations, 70 percent of workers in the same survey said that their companies cared about them, and 72 percent claimed to be happy in their jobs.

The Religious Left also refuses to acknowledge the considerable academic research showing that mandated wage hikes often eliminate the jobs of low-skilled workers—the very people whom it seeks to help. In editorials the Reverend Rebekah Jordan, a Methodist minister who heads Memphis's local interfaith group, used union-sponsored research to argue that living-wage laws benefit workers and do little harm to employment rates. But David Neumark, a researcher at the University of California at Berkeley's Institute of Business and Economics Research and one of the world's foremost authorities on wage laws, has found that while living-wage laws do boost the income of some low-wage workers, they also have "strong negative employment effects"—that is, they vaporize jobs. In one study, Neumark noted that a 50 percent boost in the living wage produced a decline in employment for the lowest-skilled workers of between 6 and 8 percent.

Further, the leftist clerics ignore the cultural underpinnings of much poverty. About two-thirds of poor families with children today are single-parent households, largely dependent on government subsidies. Single women with little education head most of these households. The kind of work for which these mothers are qualified—entry-level, low-wage—makes it hard to support large families; and the time they must devote to raising their kids makes it hard, in turn, to climb the economic ladder. In a recent study on American poverty highlighted by the National Bureau of Economic Research, economists from the University of California at Davis found that "changes in family structure—notably a doubling of the percent of families headed by a single woman—can account for a 3.7 percentage point increase in poverty rates, more than the entire rise in the poverty rate from 10.7 percent to 12.8 percent since 1980."

By contrast, observes Catholic neoconservative writer Michael Novak, research demonstrates that the way out of poverty for most Americans is to make a few simple life choices. "Some 97 percent of those who complete high school, stay married (even if not on the first try), and work full-time year-round (even at the minimum wage) are not poor," Novak points out. "Nearly all poverty in the United States is associated with the absence of one or more of these three basic accomplishments."

Gary Palmer, president of the Alabama Policy Institute, a conservative think tank, worries that leftist clerics have become part of the poverty problem. "The Religious Left has abdicated responsibility as a moral authority," says Palmer, who in 2003 faced off against religious leaders after they backed Alabama governor Bob Riley's push to raise taxes. Palmer argues that religious groups can play a significant role in fighting poverty—but only by striving to strengthen the family and personal responsibility. "The attitude of the Religious Left seems to be, 'Let government do it,' and they would drive us toward a kind of Christian socialism," he says.

Not only are the Religious Left's fuzzy, shopworn ideas out of step with the latest poverty research; they're also at odds with the opinions of many congregants. Consider the leftist clergy's latest initiative, "New Sanctuary." Opposing government efforts to deport illegal immigrants, the IWJ has helped organize a national network of congregations that grant illegal aliens sanctuary in their churches. Responding to critics who complain that religious leaders shouldn't assist lawbreakers, Bobo counters: "There is a strong belief among many people of faith that if laws are unjust, there may be times and situations in which laws should be broken."

But many American Christians don't share that belief, at least when it comes to immigration. According to a Pew Center poll, more white, mainline Protestants and non-Hispanic Catholics condemn helping illegal immigrants evade the law than condone such behavior. "Despite the strong pro-immigrant statements issued recently by a number of prominent religious leaders," Pew noted, "polls show that a large segment of the public—including many Catholics, mainline Protestants and evangelicals—harbor serious concerns about immigration and immigrants."

The dissonance between Religious Left leaders and their congregants on immigration isn't anomalous. While the NCC and its member churches pursue a variety of left-wing causes—even partnering with the activist organization MoveOn.org and featuring speakers like Michael Moore at events—a Pew poll has found that 54 percent of white, mainline Protestants and 50 percent of Catholics voted Republican in the 2004 presidential elections. Those who attended church regularly voted Republican even more heavily—at nearly the same rate as evangelical Christians, in fact.

Those numbers are a reminder that for four decades, as the leadership of America's mainline Christian churches has moved steadily leftward, those churches' memberships have declined as a percentage of the U.S. population, even as the number of Christian evangelicals exploded. Cultural issues drove most of the flight from old-line churches, which became as liberal socially as anti-capitalist economically; believers moved to more conservative congregations, whose positions on issues such as abortion and the traditional family lined up more comfortably with their own. So the left-wing clerics may be buying greater political influence with their new alliance through organized labor, but in so doing they may wind up further alienating their shrinking flock.

CHAPTER 8

The Advocates and Washington's Housing Disorders

IN THE LAST MONTH of the administration of George W. Bush, the *New York Times* published a 5,100-word article charging that Bush housing policies had "stoked" the foreclosure crisis—and thus the financial meltdown. By pushing for lax lending standards, encouraging government enterprises to make mortgages more available, and leaning on private lenders to come up with innovative ways to lend to ever more Americans—using "the mighty muscle of the federal government," as the president himself put it—Bush had lured millions of people into bad mortgages that they ultimately couldn't afford, the *Times* said.

Yet almost everything that the *Times* accused the Bush administration of doing had been pursued many times by earlier administrations, both Democratic and Republican—and often with calamitous results. Beginning with Herbert Hoover's efforts to boost homeownership and then the mortgage reforms of the Great Depression, the federal government became the biggest player in the housing business decades ago. Then, starting in the 1960s, prodded by advocacy groups, the government used that power as a tool of the War on Poverty and helped engender a long, relentless decline in mortgage standards that proved catastrophic. In ignoring this long history the *Times*'s analysis exemplified our collective amnesia about Washington's repeated attempts to expand homeownership and the disasters they've caused. The ideal of homeownership has become so sacrosanct, it seems, that we never learn from these disasters. Instead we clean them up and then—as if under some strange compulsion—set in motion the mechanisms of the next housing catastrophe.

We've largely forgotten that Herbert Hoover, as secretary of commerce, initiated the first major Washington campaign to boost homeownership after the 1920 census revealed a small drop in ownership rates. In 1922 Hoover launched the Own Your Own Home campaign, hailed at the time as unique in the nation's history, and the 1930 census would later reveal a significant elevation in ownership rates. But when the stock market crashed in October 1929 and banks around the country failed, the housing market collapsed and thousands of Americans who had been swept up in the enthusiasm Hoover generated lost their homes.

The depression-era federal government responded by creating many institutions to fix flaws in the mortgage market: the Federal Home Loan Bank system to provide a stable source of funds for banks; the Federal Housing Administration (FHA) to insure mortgages; the Federal National Mortgage Association (later known as Fannie Mae) to purchase those insured mortgages; and the Federal Savings and Loan Insurance Corporation to prevent future bank runs. These were valuable initiatives, but they meant that by the end of the Great Depression the U.S. government had become the dominant force in the mortgage market.

Politicians could now use that regulated market to advance their own policy agendas—or their careers. And almost immediately, politics took center stage. Intent on a postwar project of boosting homeownership, Congress passed the GI Bill in 1944, extending a range of benefits to returning veterans—including government-subsidized mortgages. With the feds footing a big portion of the bill, the nation's long-moribund mortgage market came alive, more than doubling in volume between 1945 and 1950. By 1949 more than half of American households owned homes, and 40 percent of the new mortgages were government subsidized. But as homeownership grew, political pressure to allow riskier loans increased too. Rising home prices, a result of a booming national economy, soon began to drive some homes out of reach for ordinary Americans, among them veterans returning from peacekeeping duties in Europe and later from fighting in Korea. Under pressure to keep meeting housing demand, the government began loosening its mortgage-lending standards—cutting the size of required down payments, approving loans with higher ratios of payments to income, and extending the terms of mortgages. But by attracting riskier home buyers, these moves provoked a surge in foreclosures on government-backed mortgages. The failure rate on FHA-insured loans spiked fivefold from 1950 to 1960, according to a 1970 National Bureau of Economic Research study, while the failure rate on mortgages made through the Veterans Administration nearly doubled over the same period.

Ignoring these problems, the government embarked on another, more serious failed attempt to increase homeownership as part of its War on Poverty effort to revive flagging cities: the FHA's urban-loan debacle, its most ruinous lending mistake yet. Riots had ripped apart Cleveland, Detroit, Los Angeles, Newark, and other cities during the mid-sixties. Politicians in both parties and advocates argued that extending the American dream of homeownership to poor blacks (especially those who'd migrated from the rural South to northeastern cities) and to immigrants (especially Puerto Ricans) would stabilize urban communities and prevent further violence. "Past experience has shown that families offered decent homes at prices they can afford have demonstrated a new dignity, a new attitude toward their jobs," said Democratic congressman Wright Patman. Or as Republican senator Charles Percy bluntly put it: "People won't burn down houses they own."

So in 1968 the federal government passed a law giving poor families FHA-insured loans that required down payments of as little as $250. Not urban uplift but urban nightmare followed. Seedy speculators began snapping up homes in transitional urban areas where crime and unemployment were rising. They would make lowball, all-cash offers to fearful residents, eager to sell and get out of the neighborhood. Once they had the properties, the speculators then turned around and used the new FHA-insured mortgages to sell the homes to low-income minority families for double or triple the price.

Many of these mortgages—approved by bribed FHA inspectors—were way beyond the buyers' means. And many buyers simply weren't prepared to become homeowners. Some didn't realize that they'd be responsible for paying utilities, property taxes, and maintenance. In some markets, like Philadelphia and Detroit, more than 20 percent of the mortgages went to single mothers on welfare. And why not, the government reasoned—they enjoyed a steady stream of government income, didn't they? This naive view ignored the growing evidence that such households suffered from family breakdown and social disorder, which made them less than ideal borrowers. Journalists also found numerous buyers who couldn't read English and had no idea what their sales contracts said.

Foreclosures spread like a horrible virus, infecting at least 20 cities. About 4,000 FHA-insured home mortgages in Philadelphia defaulted in just the three years from 1969 to 1971—more than the total number the city had seen over the previous 33 years of FHA loans. Foreclosures made the FHA Detroit's biggest homeowner, at a cost of roughly $200 million in losses. In New York a 500-count federal indictment estimated that some 7,500 FHA-backed homes in East New York, Brownsville, Bushwick, and other troubled neighborhoods had gone bust, costing upward of $300 million. In the end, the government absorbed an estimated $1.4 billion in losses nationwide.

The failed program had more than a financial cost. Neighborhoods like Bushwick—a once-stable blue-collar community in Brooklyn—fell into ruin as scores of low-income buyers simply walked away from their properties, and arsonists, an urban plague at the time, torched the vacant homes. Residents who lived near abandoned houses began sleeping on their porches with guns in their laps to ward off the arsonists. Whole blocks remained burned out for years.

Sure, speculators and corrupt inspectors had duped the FHA. But the meltdown couldn't have happened without the unexamined assumption of War on Poverty architects that homeownership would transform the lives of low-income buyers in positive ways. "The program could not work because it tried to solve a problem of wealth creation through debt creation," Harvard historian Louis Hyman recently observed, aptly comparing the FHA scandals with today's subprime crisis.

The national FHA scandal should have awakened Washington to the dangers of its homeownership promotion efforts. Instead the government, prodded by advocacy groups, simply changed its sights. Just as it had pushed the FHA to insure loans in poor neighborhoods, it now began pushing private banks to lend more in those neighborhoods. The new campaign lasted thirty years, but the outcome was—yet again—foreclosures on a massive scale. The main difference, as we know all too well, was that the foreclosures helped usher in a global financial crisis.

This time the government's spur to action was claims by housing and civil rights activists that banks were "redlining"—intentionally not lending in minority neighborhoods. In April 1975 a new group of activists, the National People's Action on Housing, brought the concept to a national audience at a Chicago conference. Over the next few years a series of studies by advocacy groups and local newspapers purported to prove that redlining was real. Black neighborhoods, the studies showed, received far fewer mortgages than mostly white areas did, and black applicants had their loans shot down more often than whites with similar incomes. Banks and academic experts responded that the studies didn't include information about the creditworthiness of borrowers in black neighborhoods, a more important factor than income. Nevertheless the media worked themselves into a frenzy, pillorying government officials who dared object to the studies' conclusions.

Congress passed a bill in 1975 requiring banks to provide the government with information on their lending activities in poor urban areas. Two years later it passed the Community Reinvestment Act (CRA), which gave regulators the power to deny banks the right to expand if they didn't lend sufficiently in those neighborhoods. In 1979 the Federal Deposit Insurance Corporation (FDIC) rocked the banking industry when it used the CRA to turn down an application by the Greater New York Savings Bank to open a branch on the Upper East Side of Manhattan. The government contended that the bank didn't lend enough in Brooklyn, its home market.

Bankers recognized that a fundamental shift in regulation was taking place. Previously the government had simply made sure that banks' practices were safe and that depositors' funds were protected. Now it would use its power over banks to shape their lending strategies. Soon after the Greater New York ruling, for instance, the Federal Home Loan Bank Board told a Toledo, Ohio, bank that it had to eliminate its practice of lending only to its current customers during times when funds were tight; the maneuver might be discriminatory. The FHLBB also cast a dubious eye on other bank actions to tighten credit in a downturn, such as raising the minimum down payment on mortgages.

Other actions sent similar messages. In 1980, the FDIC told a Maryland bank that it couldn't expand unless it started lending in the District of Columbia, even though the bank had no branches there. Soon the government was instructing wholesale banks—institutions that have no branches and typically don't lend to consumers at all—that they too had to pursue inner-city lending programs.

Next came a campaign to lower lending criteria, which, the housing advocates argued, were racist and had to change. The campaign gathered momentum in 1986 when Acorn threatened to oppose an acquisition by a Southern bank, Louisiana Bancshares, until it agreed to new "flexible credit and underwriting standards" for minority borrowers—for example, counting public assistance and food stamps as income. The next year Acorn led a coalition of advocacy groups calling for industry-wide changes in lending standards. Among the demanded reforms were the easing of minimum down-payment requirements and of the condition that borrowers have enough cash at a closing to cover two to three months of mortgage payments (research had shown that lack of money in hand was a big reason some mortgages failed quickly).

The advocates also attacked Fannie Mae, the giant quasi-government agency that bought loans from banks in order to allow them to make new loans. Its underwriters were "strictly by-the-book interpreters" of lending standards and turned down purchases of unconventional loans, charged Acorn. The pressure eventually paid off. In 1992 Congress passed legislation requiring Fannie Mae and the similar Freddie Mac to devote 30 percent of their loan purchases to mortgages for low- and moderate-income borrowers.

The campaign gained further traction with the election of Bill Clinton, whose housing secretary, Henry Cisneros, declared that he would expand homeownership among lower- and lower-middle-income renters. His strategy: pushing for no-down-payment loans; expanding the size of mortgages that the government would insure against losses; and using the CRA and other lending laws to direct more private money into low-income programs. Shortly after Cisneros announced his plan, Fannie Mae and Freddie Mac agreed to begin buying loans under new, looser guidelines. Freddie Mac, for instance, started approving low-income buyers with bad credit histories or none at all, as long as they were current on rent and utilities payments. Freddie Mac also said it would begin counting income from seasonal jobs and public assistance toward its income minimum, despite the FHA disaster of the sixties.

To meet their goals, the two mortgage giants enlisted large lenders—including nonbanks, which weren't covered by the CRA—in the effort. Freddie Mac began an "alternative qualifying" program with the Sears Mortgage Corporation that let a borrower qualify for a loan with a monthly payment as high as 50 percent of his income, at a time when most private mortgage companies wouldn't exceed 33 percent. The program also allowed borrowers with bad credit to get mortgages if they took credit-counseling classes administered by Acorn and other nonprofits. Subsequent research would show that such classes have little impact on default rates.

Pressuring nonbank lenders to make more loans to poor minorities didn't stop with Sears. If it didn't happen, Clinton officials warned, they'd seek to extend CRA regulations to *all* mortgage makers. In Congress, Representative Maxine Waters called financial firms not covered by the CRA "among the most egregious redliners." To rebuff the criticism, the Mortgage Bankers Association (MBA) shocked the financial world by signing a 1994 agreement with the Department of Housing and Urban Development (HUD), pledging to increase lending to minorities and join in new efforts to rewrite lending standards. The first MBA member to sign up: Countrywide Financial, the mortgage firm that would be at the core of the subprime meltdown.

As the volume of lending to low-income borrowers increased, the CRA and the loan business it spurred became big business for the country's nonprofits, many of whom were enlisted by banks under pressure to run loan counseling programs for the poor or to direct inner-city residents to loans. A 2000 study by a U.S. Senate subcommittee estimated that CRA had directed some $9.5 billion from banks to nonprofits.

Acorn became especially expert at exploiting the law. In 1993 Acorn crafted a $55 million, eleven-city lending program administered by it and financed by fourteen major banks eager to avoid CRA woes. In 1998 Acorn activists disrupted Federal Reserve hearings on the proposed Citicorp merger with Travelers, waving red umbrellas, a corporate symbol of Travelers, and then later protested Citigroup's acquisition of Associates First Capital Corp. Eventually Citigroup signed an agreement to provide mortgages through Acorn counseling centers, including home loans to undocumented aliens in California.

But the long effort to reduce lending standards ultimately spread far beyond nonprofit groups. Slowly the mortgage industry, which had been prodded to weaken its lending standards, began pitching loans with the same language that the government and activists had long used, and promoting the same debased lending standards. A 1998 sales pitch by a Bear Stearns managing director advised banks to begin packaging their loans to low-income borrowers into securities that the firm could sell, according to Stan Liebowitz, a professor of economics at the University of Texas who unearthed the pitch. Forget traditional underwriting standards when considering these loans, the director advised. For a low-income borrower, he continued in all-too-familiar terms, owning a home was "a near-sacred obligation. A family will do almost anything to meet that monthly mortgage payment." Bunk, says Liebowitz: "The claim that lower-income homeowners are somehow different in their devotion to their home is a purely emotional claim with no evidence to support it."

By the late 1990s lenders, keen to find new markets to tap, had jumped completely on board the low-income-mortgage bandwagon. In 1997 homeownership had reached a new high of 66 percent of households. That meant that many, even most, creditworthy households had already made the plunge. The biggest opportunities for new business thus seemed to be lower-income borrowers. "We believe that low-income borrowers are going to be our leading customers going into the twenty-first century," an executive for Norwest Mortgage, a Maryland lender, told the trade press in 1998. With Fannie Mae and Freddie Mac footing some of the bill, "banks are buying these loans from us as fast as we can originate them."

Any concern that regulators should tighten standards as the loan volume expanded was quickly dismissed. When in early 2000 the FDIC proposed increasing capital requirements for lenders making "subprime" loans—loans to people with questionable credit, that is—Democratic representative Carolyn Maloney of New York told a congressional hearing that she feared that the step would dry up CRA loans. Her fellow New York Democrat John J. LaFalce urged regulators "not to be premature" in imposing new regulations.

And even with lenders now chasing this market enthusiastically, the Clinton administration kept pushing for higher government-mandated goals. In July 1999, HUD proposed new levels for Fannie Mae's and Freddie Mac's low-income lending; in September, Fannie Mae agreed to begin purchasing loans made to "borrowers with slightly impaired credit"—that is, with credit standards even lower than the government had been pushing for a generation.

Congress and the Bush administration later took up where Clinton left off. Not content that nearly seven in ten American households owned their own homes, legislators in 2004 pressed new affordable-housing goals on the two mortgage giants, which through 2007 purchased some $1 trillion in loans to lower- and moderate-income buyers. The buying spree helped spark a massive increase in securitization of mortgages to people with dubious credit. To carry out this mission, Fannie Mae turned to old friends, like Angelo Mozilo of Countrywide, which became the biggest supplier of mortgages to low-income buyers for Fannie Mae to purchase.

Executives at these firms won hosannas. Harvard University's Joint Center for Housing Studies invited Mozilo to give its prestigious 2003 Dunlop Lecture. Subject: "The American Dream of Homeownership: From Cliché to Mission." *La Opinión*, a Spanish-language newspaper, dubbed Countrywide its Corporation of the Year. Meantime, in Congress, Waters praised the "outstanding leadership" of Fannie Mae chairman Franklin Raines.

There was never any shortage of evidence that the new loans were much riskier than conventional mortgages. In October 1994, Fannie Mae head James Johnson had reminded a banking convention that mortgages with small down payments had a much higher risk of defaulting. (A Duff & Phelps study found that they were nearly three times more likely to default than conventional mortgages.) Yet the very next month, Fannie Mae said it expected to back loans to low-income home buyers with a 97 percent loan-to-value ratio—that is, loans in which the buyer puts down just 3 percent—as part of a commitment, made earlier that year to Congress, to purchase $1 trillion in affordable-housing mortgages by the end of the nineties. According to Edward Pinto, who served as the company's chief credit officer, the program was the result of political pressure on Fannie Mae that trumped lending standards.

An Atlanta-area minority loan program, crafted hastily by banks and advocacy groups after a newspaper redlining exposé, provided further evidence. The program lent more than half its mortgages to single women with children, including women on public assistance, some of whom took on payments of up to 50 percent of their monthly income. Within a year, 10 percent of the loans had gone delinquent and the homeowners were sinking deeper into other kinds of debt. Yet the program's woes received little publicity. Community groups argued that the difficulties were all the fault of the banks, which should have offered the loans with lower interest rates.

What made it easier to dismiss such ominous failures was that some of the nation's most prestigious financial regulators and researchers, including the Federal Reserve Bank of Boston, got behind the movement to loosen lending standards. In 1992 the Boston Fed produced an extraordinary twenty-nine-page document that codified the new lending wisdom. Conventional mortgage criteria, the report argued, might be "unintentionally biased" because they didn't take into account "the economic culture of urban, lower-income and nontraditional customers." Lenders should thus consider junking the industry's traditional income-to-payments ratio and stop viewing an applicant's "lack of credit history" as a "negative factor." Further, if applicants had bad credit, banks should "consider extenuating circumstances"—even though a study by mortgage insurance companies would soon show, not surprisingly, that borrowers with no credit rating or a bad one were far more likely to default. If applicants didn't have enough savings for a down payment, the Boston Fed urged, banks should allow loans from nonprofits or government assistance agencies to count toward one. A later study of Freddie Mac mortgages would find that a borrower who made a down payment with third-party funds was four times more likely to default, a reminder that traditional underwriting standards weren't arbitrary but based on historical lending patterns.

Another reason government kept up the pressure was that no matter how high ownership rates climbed, there was always a group below the norm that needed help. The country's substantial immigration rates in the 1990s and early 2000s, for instance, produced a whole new cadre of potential Latino borrowers. To serve them, the Congressional Hispanic Caucus launched Hogar, an initiative that pushed for easing lending standards for immigrants, including touting so-called seller-financed mortgages in which a builder provided down-payment aid to buyers via contributions to nonprofit groups, an initiative the IRS later said was little more than a blatant tax dodge. As a result, mortgage lending to Hispanics soared. Once the foreclosure crisis hit in 2007, in districts where Hispanics make up at least 25 percent of the population foreclosure rates soared nearly 50 percent higher than the national average, according to a *Wall Street Journal* analysis.

That a blatantly deceptive technique like seller-financed down payments would lie at the heart of a nonprofit-operated mortgage program sponsored by a congressional caucus was representative of the larger problem that decades of efforts by government to expand

and subsidize homeownership produced. As Washington prodded institutions like Fannie Mae and Freddie Mac to buy up more and more mortgages, an "at any cost" mentality came to dominate the entire market, especially as the pool of qualified applicants shrank. By 2000, applicants routinely came to lie about their assets and incomes. Real estate agents sent clients with problematic credit or income histories to mortgage banks they knew were likely to look the other way at questionable applications. Knowing they had a willing buyer for their mortgages in Fannie and Freddie, banks like Washington Mutual churned out mortgage volume by telling their loan officers that "a thin file [of documents from mortgage applicants] was a good file." These problems accelerated especially after Fannie and Freddie were told once again, in 1999, to commit to new affordable lending goals.

From 2001 through 2007, according to the FBI, reports of mortgage fraud soared tenfold nationwide. No one knows precisely how deep the problem ran, but some mortgage servicers, examining portfolios of subprime mortgages that went bad in 2007, found that up to 70 percent of them had involved some kind of misrepresentation. Loans that required no verification of the borrower's income infamously became known as "liar loans." One mortgage lender who compared one hundred of these loans with IRS tax filings found that in 60 percent of cases the applicants exaggerated their incomes (or underreported them to the IRS). Occupancy fraud, in which investors intent on buying new homes and then quickly flipping them for a profit lied about their intentions, accounted for about 20 percent of all fraudulent mortgage applications.

Washington's, indeed America's, housing obsession—decades of government and advocacy-group efforts to water down underwriting standards, private mortgage makers' desire to find new pools of customers as homeownership rates rose, and the rapid growth of securitization of risky loans—carried a steep cost. When the Federal Reserve added low interest rates and plenty of financial liquidity to the mix, the housing boom became a bubble which included possibly millions of mortgages made under dubious circumstances and ripe for failure. And then, as everyone knows, the bubble burst in 2007, leading to economic disaster. And though lenders made risky loans to borrowers across the income spectrum, many of the failing mortgages were in lower- and lower-middle-income neighborhoods, just as with the FHA program of the 1960s. A Federal Reserve Bank of New York study of foreclosures in New Jersey, the state in its region hit hardest by the mortgage collapse, revealed that zip codes with the worst rates were mostly in areas where household income was "concentrated at the lower end of the household income range."

Yet before we had even worked our way through this crisis, elected officials and policymakers were busy readying the next. Barney Frank, the Massachusetts congressman who serves as chair of the House Financial Services Committee, balked in 2009 at proposals to privatize Fannie Mae and Freddie Mac, which would eliminate their risk to taxpayers and their susceptibility to political machinations. Why? Simple: the government uses them to subsidize the affordable-housing programs that Frank supports. California congressman Joe Baca, head of the

Congressional Hispanic Caucus in 2009, also opposed reining in affordable housing lending. "We need to keep credit easily accessible to our minority communities," he asserted.

Changing notions of fairness and equity over the years had clouded policymakers' minds. Our praiseworthy initial efforts—to eliminate housing discrimination and provide all Americans an equal *opportunity* to buy a home—were eventually turned on their heads by politicians, who instead tried to ensure equality of *outcomes*. Advocacy groups like Acorn, meanwhile, pushed for higher ownership rates and more subsidies because they were allowed to engineer many of these programs. And so, for instance, when elected officials learned that fewer than 50 percent of Hispanic households in America owned homes, Latino politicians sponsored a campaign to raise ownership. Yet the lower rate was perfectly understandable, given the average lower household incomes and shorter tenure in the country of Latinos, compared with the average American household.

What principles, then, should govern federal policy toward homeownership and the housing construction market? First, our experience since the Great Depression teaches us that a rising economy, not subsidies and advocacy programs, is the best and safest way to boost homeownership. By some estimates, the "natural" rate of homeownership in America, without dicey government-enabled mortgages, would still be nearly 65 percent—among the highest rates in the world. Government's most important role in the market should be to ensure a sturdy economy and a reliable judicial system that protects the interests of buyers and sellers in what is the largest transaction that most will ever undertake.

Ultimately the goal should be to end subsidies that allow government a disproportionate role in housing policy, because that will always leave the market open to politicization. It is one thing when politicians, prodded by big-government advocates, sponsor programs like community development grants that are ineffective and waste tax dollars. But when the government extended the dependency mentality of the War on Poverty to housing, it enabled something far greater than just wasteful spending. Its political meddling in this vast marketplace helped to wreak havoc in the economy.

CHAPTER 9

A Culture of Entitlement Everywhere

THE GENIUS OF AMERICA in the early nineteenth century, observed Alexis de Tocqueville, was that its citizens pursued "productive industry" but did not allow themselves to be "carried away, and lose all self-restraint" in the quest for riches. Instead Americans at the time generally maintained "the close connection which exists between the private fortune of each of them and the prosperity of all." Behind America's balancing act, the pioneering French social thinker noted, lay a common set of civic virtues that celebrated not merely hard work but also thrift, integrity, self-reliance, and modesty. Some seventy-five years later, the sociologist Max Weber dubbed the qualities that Tocqueville observed the "Protestant ethic" and considered them the cornerstone of successful capitalism. Like Tocqueville, Weber saw that ethic most fully realized in America. Preached by luminaries like

Benjamin Franklin, taught in public schools, embodied in popular novels, repeated in self-improvement books, and transmitted to immigrants, it undergirded and promoted America's success.

What would Tocqueville or Weber think of America today? In place of thrift they would find a nation of debtors, some staggering beneath loans obtained under false pretenses. In place of a steady, patient accumulation of wealth they would find bankers and financiers with such a short-term perspective that they never paused to consider the consequences or risks of selling securities they didn't understand. In place of a country where all a man asks of government is "not to be disturbed in his toil," as Tocqueville put it, they would find a nation of rent-seekers demanding government subsidies to purchase homes, start new ventures, or bail out old ones. And they would find a political dynamic not simply about Left versus Right or Democrat versus Republican, but one that is often about the public sector and its perks versus the private economy.

And they would understand why. After flourishing for three centuries, the American ethic that Tocqueville and Weber identified began to disintegrate, with key elements slowly disappearing from modern American society, vanishing from schools, from business, from popular culture, and most especially from government, and leaving us with an economic system unmoored from the restraints of civic virtue. Not even Adam Smith—who was a moral philosopher, after all—imagined capitalism operating in such an ethical vacuum.

The American experiment that Tocqueville chronicled in the 1830s was more than just an effort to see if men could live without a monarch and govern themselves. A free society had to be one in which people could pursue economic opportunity with only minimal interference from the state. To do so without producing anarchy required a self-discipline that was, to Max Weber, the core of the capitalist ethic. "The impulse to acquisition, pursuit of gain, of money, of the greatest possible amount of money, has in itself nothing to do with capitalism," Weber wrote in *The Protestant Ethic and the Spirit of Capitalism*. "Unlimited greed for gain is not in the least identical with capitalism, and still less its spirit." Instead the essence of capitalism was "a rational tempering" of the impulse to accumulate wealth so as to keep a business (and ultimately the whole economy) sustainable and self-renewing, Weber wrote. It was "the pursuit of profit, and forever renewed profit, by means of continuous, rational . . . enterprise."

Weber famously argued that the Protestant Reformation—with John Calvin's and Martin Luther's emphasis on individual responsibility, hard work, thrift, providence, honesty, and deferred gratification at its center—shaped the spirit of capitalism and helped it succeed. And nowhere did the fusing of capitalism and the virtues that made up the work ethic find a fuller expression than in America, where Puritan pioneers founded settlements animated by a Calvinist dedication to work. One result was a remarkable society in which, as Tocqueville would observe, all "honest callings are honorable" and in which "the notion of labor is therefore presented to the mind on every side as the necessary, natural, and honest condition of human existence." Unlike in Europe, where aristocrats and gentry often scorned labor, in the United

States "a wealthy man thinks that he owes it to public opinion to devote his leisure to some kind of industrial or commercial pursuit, or to public business. He would think himself in bad repute if he employed his life solely in living."

This thick and complex American ethic, so essential to the success of the early, struggling American settlements, became part of the country's civic fabric. It found its most succinct expression in the writings of Benjamin Franklin, whose well-known maxims, now considered quaintly old-fashioned, recommended to citizens of the new country a worldview that promoted work and the patient pursuit of wealth. Franklin's ideas, widely applauded, permeated popular culture and education. The leading grammar school textbooks of the nineteenth century, by William Holmes McGuffey and his brother Alexander, inculcated children with the virtues of work and thrift. So did the enormously popular rags-to-riches novels of Horatio Alger, Jr., who sold some 200 million books with plotlines that are a road map of the American ethic. The work ethic even shaped American play. The most popular game of its time, "The Checkered Game of Life," produced by Milton Bradley in the mid-nineteenth century and sold door-to-door, challenged players to travel through life and earn points for successfully completing school, getting married, and working hard while avoiding pitfalls like gambling and idleness. Later this ethic served as a lodestar for millions of poor immigrants, many from countries with little experience of free markets and democracy, whose assimilation into a culture they recognized as American reinvigorated the country, helping to set late-nineteenth- and early-twentieth-century America on a distinctly different path from much of Europe.

The breakup of this three-hundred-year-old consensus began with the cultural protests of the 1960s, which questioned and discarded many traditional virtues. The roots of these objections lay in what Daniel Bell described in *The Cultural Contradictions of Capitalism* as the rejection of traditional bourgeois qualities by late-nineteenth-century European artists and intellectuals who sought "to substitute for religion or morality an aesthetic justification of life." By the 1960s that modernist tendency had evolved into a credo of self-fulfillment in which "nothing is forbidden, all is to be explored," Bell wrote. Out went a common consensus that the virtues of prudence, thrift, temperance, self-discipline, and deferral of gratification were desirable.

Weakened along with all these virtues that made up the American work ethic was Americans' belief in the value of work itself. Along with "turning on" and "tuning in," the sixties protesters also "dropped out." As the editor of the 1973 *American Work Ethic* noted, "affluence, hedonism and radicalism" turned many Americans away from work and the pursuit of career advancement, resulting in a sharp slowdown in U.S. productivity from 1965 through 1970. So great a transformation of values was occurring that, as George Bloom of MIT's Sloan School of Management wrote in a 1971 essay on America's declining work ethic, "It is unfortunate but true that 'progress' is becoming a bad word in virtually all sectors of society."

In this era, being virtuous became something separate from work. When the Milton Bradley Company reintroduced "The Checkered Game of Life" in a modern version called "The Game of Life" in the mid-1960s, it abandoned the notion of rewarding traditional bourgeois virtues like completing an education or marrying. What was left of the game was simply the pursuit of cash, until Milton Bradley, criticized for this version, redesigned the game to include rewards for doing good. But its efforts produced mere political correctness: in the new version, recycling trash and contributing to save an endangered species were virtuous actions that won a player points. Such gestures, along with tolerance and sensitivity, expanded like a gas to fill the vacuum where the traditional American ethic used to be.

The cultural upheavals of the sixties spurred deep changes in institutions—especially the schools. University education departments began to tell future grammar school teachers that they should replace the traditional teacher-centered curriculum, aimed at producing educated citizens who embraced a common American ethic, with a new, child-centered approach that treated every pupil's "personal development" as different and special. During the 1960s, when intellectuals and college students dismissed traditional American values as oppressive barriers to fulfillment, grammar schools generally jettisoned the traditional curriculum. "Education professors eagerly joined New Left professors to promote the idea that any top-down imposition of any curriculum would be a right-wing plot designed to perpetuate the dominant white, male, bourgeois power structure," writes education reformer E. D. Hirsch, Jr., in his *The Making of Americans: Democracy and Our Schools*.

This change in attitudes made its way into government social policy, too. The nineteenth- and early-twentieth-century notion of charity as a largely private endeavor which attempted to offer people "a hand up, not a hand out" was replaced by the idea that government had a duty to look after the poor, who were victims of a system arrayed against them. As two architects of the War on Poverty, Edward M. Kaitz and Herbert Harvey Hyman, argued in their book *Urban Planning for Social Welfare*, it was time to abandon America's outdated bourgeois values which directed aid only to the "deserving" poor. And so our welfare system, begun during the Great Depression as temporary aid to orphans and widows, became a program of lifetime assistance. Welfare rolls soared as America witnessed the growth of a permanent underclass and the concomitant growth of a permanent class of government-financed social-services groups serving the poor.

Discarding the bourgeois values that had helped sustain Weber's "rational tempering" of the impulse to accumulate wealth had far more widespread consequences. When the schools and the wider society demoted them, the effects were predictable. In schools, for instance, the new "every child is special" curriculum prompted a sharp uptick in students' self-absorption, according to psychologists Jean M. Twenge and W. Keith Campbell in *The Narcissism Epidemic: Living in the Age of Entitlement*. Thus did the sixties generation spawn the Me Generation of the seventies. By the mid-1980s a poll of teens found that more than nine in ten listed shopping as their favorite pastime.

The economic shocks that followed the tumultuous late 1960s, especially the devastating inflation of the

1970s, reinforced an emerging materialism. Thanks to the Johnson administration's illusion that the country could finance massive social-welfare programs and a war without consequences, the United States by 1974 staggered under double-digit annual inflation gains. The inflation hit hardest those who had embraced the work ethic, destroying lifetimes of savings in unprecedented price spikes and sending the message that "saving and shunning debt was for saps," *Fortune* observed. "The lesson seemed to be, buy, buy, buy, before the money visibly crumbling to dust in your hand vanishes completely."

Once Fed chairman Paul Volcker's tight-money policy tamed inflation in the early 1980s, America began to pick itself up. But it was a different country, one that had lost to some degree the "rational tempering" of the "pursuit of gain," and where a notion of entitlement that had infected government policy and programs for the poor came increasingly to be reflected in middle- and upper-class attitudes too. The corporate restructurings of the 1980s, prompted by a new generation of risk-taking entrepreneurs and takeover artists who used aggressive financial instruments with provocative names like "junk bonds" to buy and then make over big companies, shook corporate America out of its 1970s complacency. But the plant closings, downsizings, and restructurings of the 1980s also stoked anxiety among workers. While the results were often salutary for the firms, the "get it while you can" mentality that developed among some workers and investors found its ultimate expression in the "day traders" of the technology stock boom, speculators with a "right now" time horizon.

Even worse, some Americans came to believe that succeeding in life was an insider game in which the government was complicit. When a big American bank, Continental Illinois, which had made risky investments, was about to collapse in 1984, the government took the unprecedented step of moving in to save it, guaranteeing not only the money of depositors but also the investments of bondholders, and in the process promoting the notion that some financial institutions would be saved no matter how reckless their business practices. Later, when Wall Street takeover-era titans Michael Milken and Ivan Boesky pleaded guilty to insider-trading charges, their confessions strengthened a growing sense that a new ethic had superseded the old standard of playing by the rules. The 1980s version of the Horatio Alger tales became not an inspiring story of uplift but the popular movie *Wall Street*, with Gordon Gekko's infamous "greed is good" speech.

With government policy reinforcing the "get it now" mentality, a new era of consumption based on credit blossomed in the resurgent 1980s, and Americans turned from savers to debtors. Ostentatious displays of wealth grew more common. From 1982, the year that Volcker finally tamed inflation, to 1986, luxury-car sales doubled in America. The average age of a purchaser of a fur coat—that ultimate status symbol—in the mid-1980s declined from fifty to just twenty-six. To fuel such purchases, inflation-adjusted total U.S. consumer-credit debt rose nearly threefold, to $2.56 trillion from 1980 to 2008, while the nation's savings rate shrank from an average of about 12 percent of personal income annually in the early 1980s to less than 1 percent by 2005. Some middle-class Americans came to resemble not the thrifty bourgeoisie of the early Industrial Revolution but the landed gentry of that era who drained their real estate for cash to fund lavish living. One stark illustration of the change: by 2006 those who refinanced their mortgages were taking out in cash nearly a quarter of the equity they'd accumulated—compared with just 5 percent a decade earlier. A big reason Americans' debt was growing, in other words, was that they were borrowing against their rapidly appreciating assets as fast as they grew. The denouement of this transformation was the 2008 meltdown of world financial markets. America has certainly had its con artists, robber barons, and speculators before, but what distinguished the panic was that millions of mortgages belonging to ordinary Americans triggered it—mortgages that were foolhardy at best and fraudulent at worst.

There is little doubt that government policy, motivated by a fundamental shift in American values that ultimately deemed homeownership a "right" or entitlement rather than a goal to be pursued, helped engender this meltdown. Although housing advocates and politicians like Representative Barney Frank have claimed repeatedly that government had nothing to do with the 2008 housing meltdown, a mountain of evidence says otherwise, as I outlined in Chapter 8. No one in the private mortgage industry in the 1970s and 1980s was advocating or considering lowering mortgage standards. The entire push for new sets of inferior standards, which ultimately made mortgages available to millions of unqualified applicants, came first from advocacy groups and later from government regulators and from politicians. When banks and other players in the mortgage market resisted these new standards, citing decades of research which showed that foreclosures inevitably rose as underwriting values declined, they were branded "redliners" and "racists." Government regulators like the Federal Reserve Bank of Boston even tried to justify these charges by producing assurances that the lesser standards were indeed safe, even when there was little actual evidence of this.

Over time a generation of bankers came to believe that if these mortgages were indeed safe and even "prime" for lower-income buyers, they were safe for everyone. By the late 1990s key players in the mortgage meltdown like Bear Stearns were pitching mortgage-backed securities to investors using the same assurances the government regulators had made to bankers a decade earlier. With the government creating most of the demand for this market (in 2004 alone Fannie Mae and Freddie Mac bought 44 percent of all securities based on subprime mortgages), gradually it seemed as if virtually no mortgage was inappropriate. Weber's notion of a rational pursuit of profits in a self-sustaining economic model went out the window.

Nothing illustrates this more strikingly than the way key players in the financial industry ultimately destroyed themselves and shattered an entire industry. The fall of America's sixth-largest bank, Washington Mutual, which built an empire based on reckless lending, exemplifies these failings. As the housing boom heated up and Fannie and Freddie snapped up loans voraciously, WaMu raced after the action at all costs. Its supervisors chastised loan officers who tried to verify suspicious claims on mortgage applications. Executives gave loan officers flyers that said,

"A thin file is a good file," according to testimony by former employees. The lender set up phone banks, like penny-stock boiler-room operations, to sell home-equity loans. Ultimately, swamped by more than $11 billion in bad loans, WaMu was seized by the federal government and sold to JPMorgan Chase, an object lesson in what Weber called the pursuit of "irrationally speculative opportunities," which undermines capitalism rather than nourishes it.

Needless to say, this is not what Weber or Adam Smith had in mind. Smith laid the groundwork for the economic theories of *The Wealth of Nations* in his preceding book, *The Theory of Moral Sentiments*, which traces the evolution of ethics from man's nature as a social being who feels shame if he does something that he believes a neutral observer would consider improper. Smith proposed that as societies evolve, they form institutions—courts of law, for instance—that reflect and codify these ethical perceptions of individuals, and that these institutions provide the essential backbone of any sophisticated commercial system.

Modern experiments in neuroscience have tended to confirm Smith's notion that our virtues derive from our empathy for others, though with an important qualification: the ethics of individuals need reinforcement from social institutions and can be undermined by the wrong societal message, as the neuroeconomist Paul Zak writes in *Moral Markets: The Critical Role of Values in the Economy*. When people find themselves bombarded by the wrong message—like the Washington Mutual employees whose supervisors constantly pushed them into riskier and riskier actions—some will resign in disgust, but others will gradually suppress what scientists call the brain's "other-regarding" behavior and the shame that goes along with it, and violate their own ethics.

This mechanism of deception pervaded the recent housing bubble. Mortgages became so commonplace that cheaters—from applicants to the loan officers who approved blatantly unworthy applications—barely seemed to perceive that they were committing fraud. A vivid case in point is *New York Times* economics reporter Edmund Andrews's remarkable confessional tale, "My Personal Credit Crisis." Andrews relates how he obtained a mortgage under dubious circumstances, aided by a broker who encouraged him to lie on his credit applications and a lender that, when its underwriters caught his intended deception, nonetheless allowed him to apply for another, riskier kind of mortgage. When he wins the loan, Andrews admits to feeling that he has "done something bad" but also feeling "kind of cool" for making such a big score. Eventually he defaults, and his lender pays the price for its own reckless disregard for standards when it collapses and is seized by the government. All the same, society seems to reinforce Andrews's lack of shame: he received a contract to detail his credit woes in a provocatively titled book, *Busted: Life Inside the Great Mortgage Meltdown.*

In the wake of the market crash, our national discussion about how to fix capitalism seems limited to those who believe that more government will fix the problem and those who think that free markets will fix themselves. Few have asked whether we can recapture the civic virtues that nourished our commerce for three hundred years.

We're not likely to find many churches preaching those virtues today. Although America is more religious than most industrialized countries, today's pulpits hardly resound with the bourgeois ethic of hard work, thrift, and self-restraint. While the founder of Methodism, John Wesley, once observed that religion produces "industry and frugality," and the American Congregationalist preacher Henry Ward Beecher declared that the way to avoid poverty was through "provident care, and foresight, and industry and frugality," today the National Council of Churches, to which these denominations belong, advocates for a left-wing "social gospel" of redistributing wealth that is the culture of big-government entitlement written large. And though the Catholic church once strove to assimilate generations of poor immigrants into American economic life, today its major social-welfare organization, Catholic Charities, has become an arm of the redistributionist welfare state. Even our evangelical churches, whose theology most resembles that of the great Protestant reformers, have focused their energies primarily on social issues, such as fighting abortion, or even inveighing against welfare reform that encourages single mothers to return to work.

Could the schools do what they once did—create educated citizens inculcated with the ethical foundations of a free market? That would require rededicating the schools to "making Americans," as E. D. Hirsch proposes. Promisingly, a few public and private schools around the country have replaced the child-centered curriculum with one focused on learning about our culture and its institutions.

Hirsch's "Core Knowledge" curriculum, for instance, introduces kindergartners to the Pilgrims, Independence Day, and George Washington; first graders to Ben Franklin and the concept of law in society; and second graders to the Constitution as the foundation of our democracy. Other school reformers, according to David Whitman in *Sweating the Small Stuff*, a book about successful inner-city schools, have raised the achievement of low-income kids by using a "no excuses" model that teaches bourgeois "virtues like diligence, politeness, cleanliness, and thrift." But these examples amount only to a tiny handful, swimming against the educational mainstream.

Late in life, Adam Smith noted that government institutions can never tame and regulate a society whose citizens are not schooled in a common set of virtues. "What institution of government could tend so much to promote the happiness of mankind as the general prevalence of wisdom and virtue?" he wrote. "All government is but an imperfect remedy for the deficiency of these."

America in the twenty-first century is learning that lesson.

Index

A NOTE ON THE AUTHOR

Steven Malanga is a senior fellow at the Manhattan Institute in New York City and a contributing editor of *City Journal*, where he writes about the intersection of urban economies, business communities, and public policy. Born in Newark, New Jersey, he grew up there and studied at St. Vincent's College and at the University of Maryland. For fourteen years he was with *Crain's New York Business*, the last seven as executive editor and as a weekly columnist. He has also written *The New New Left*, and his articles have appeared in the *Wall Street Journal*, the *New York Times*, the *New York Daily News*, the *New York Post*, and other publications. He is married with a daughter and lives in West Orange, New Jersey.